T0191367

FOOD PLANTS OF INTERIOR FIRST PEOPLES

ROYAL BC MUSEUM HANDBOOK

FOOD PLANTS

OF INTERIOR FIRST PEOPLES

NANCY J. TURNER

ROYAL **BC** MUSEUM
Victoria, Canada

Text © 1997 by the Royal British Columbia Museum and the First Peoples' Cultural Foundation.
Reprinted in 2007, 2017, 2021.

Reprints in 2007 and later are published by Royal BC Museum, 675 Belleville Street, Victoria, British Columbia, V8W 9W2, Canada.

All rights reserved. No part of this book may be reproduced or transmitted in any form by any means without permission in writing from the publisher, except by a reviewer, who may quote brief passages in a review.

See page 215 for credits and copyright information for photographs and other material used in this book.

Printed in Canada.

For information on all Royal BC Museum publications, programs and exhibitions, visit our website: www.royalbcmuseum.bc.ca

Library and Archives Canada Cataloguing in Publication Data Turner, Nancy J., 1947-

Food plants of interior First Peoples

(Royal BC Museum handbook)

Previously issued 1997 by UBC Press for the Royal British Columbia Museum.
Includes bibliographical references: p.
ISBN 978-0-7726-5846-3

1. Indians of North America – Food – British Columbia – Handbooks, manuals, etc. 2. Wild plants, Edible – British Columbia – Handbooks, manuals, etc. 3. Indians of North America – Ethnobotany – British Columbia – Handbooks, manuals, etc. 4. Ethnobotany – British Columbia – Handbooks, manuals, etc. 5. Plants – British Columbia – Handbooks, manuals, etc. I. Royal BC Museum.

E78.B9 T87 2007   581.6'32089970711   C2007-960195-2

CONTENTS

PREFACE TO THE FIRST EDITION

This is the second of two volumes on food plants of British Columbian First Peoples. The first covers the coastal groups (see the table on page 17) while this volume explores the food plants used by the various groups of the interior.

I learned much of the information on gathering and preparing foods from elderly members of contemporary aboriginal communities. My field research on plant uses by interior First Peoples began in 1972 with the Fraser River Stl'atl'imx and has continued to the present, covering the Pemberton Stl'atl'imx (Lil'wat), Nlaka'pamux, Okanagan, Ktunaxa and, peripherally, Secwepemc. I owe a tremendous debt of gratitude to the many aboriginal people who generously contributed their time and knowledge to these studies. I would especially like to thank Sam Mitchell of Fountain (near Lillooet), Martina LaRochelle of Lillooet, Charlie Mack Seymour and Baptiste Ritchie of Mount Currie, Annie York of Spuzzum, Louis Phillips of Lytton, Selina Timoyakin and Larry Pierre of Penticton, Martin Louie of Oliver, Harry Robinson of Keremeos, Mr and Mrs Willie Armstrong of Penticton, Eliza Archie of Canim Lake, Aimee August of Chase, Mary Paul and Frank Whitehead of St Mary's Mission, Cranbrook, and Catherine Grevelle of Tobacco Plains. To all of these people I dedicate this book. I hope that they, their children, and their grandchildren will enjoy reading it and reliving some past pleasures.

I am also indebted to Randy Bouchard and Dorothy Kennedy of the British Columbia Indian Language Project (BCILP), Victoria, for providing additional information on plant foods of the Pemberton Stl'atl'imx, Okanagan, Chase Secwepemc and Nlaka'pamux peoples from their field research, to Dr S. McNeary for permitting me to use his field notes on Nisga'a plant uses, and to Dr B. Carlson and R. May for providing information on Kalispel and Spokane plant uses.

My field research was facilitated by the generous assistance of Randy

Bouchard, Dorothy Kennedy, Dr and Mrs L.C. Thompson, Dr A. Kuipers, Dr Jan van Eijk and Dr Larry Morgan. Kathleen Cowen, my research assistant, was extremely helpful in all stages of the preparation of this book. Dr G.W. Douglas and Gloria Douglas kindly identified some of my field collections. I gratefully acknowledge the encouragement and editorial advice of Dr A.F. Szczawinski (former Curator of Botany at the British Columbia Provincial Museum), Harold Hosford and R. Yorke Edwards (Director of the British Columbia Provincial Museum).

N.J.T.
1978

PREFACE TO THE SECOND EDITION

This is the second of the set of my two handbooks on traditional plant foods to be revised and re-issued. The original set was called *Food Plants of British Columbia Indians* and the individual volumes were titled *Part 1: Coastal Peoples* (published in 1975) and *Part 2: Interior Peoples* (1978). The first volume was re-issued in 1995 as *Food Plants of Coastal First Peoples*. This book replaces the second volume.

It is not an easy task to revise a book written nearly 20 years ago. Reading over the original preface evoked many pleasurable memories of harvesting expeditions and conversations over plant samples, delicious food and cups of tea. It made me sad, though, to realize how many friends and teachers who contributed to the first edition had passed away. Almost all of the elderly people acknowledged in the Preface to the First Edition are no longer living. But their rich knowledge lives on. All of them were teachers, not just to me, but to their families and communities. Because of them and many others like them, people still remember the past and still enjoy the traditional foods of former generations. Newer generations of elders continue to participate in the harvest, and teach their own children and grandchildren about the good foods of the land. Aboriginal leaders, educators and community members are continuing to work towards more control over and use of their own traditional lands and resources, so that the food and other products yielded by the land will continue to play a vital role in peoples' lives.

A number of people who harvest traditional food have commented that their lands were, in a way, just like the planted vegetable gardens and orchards of the European newcomers. You could find growing wild all the equivalents of a garden's harvest – potatoes, carrots, celery, berries, nuts – all there for the people to gather and use. Ecologists, anthropologists, ethnobiologists and resource managers are beginning to pay closer attention to traditional knowledge and resource management systems. They are finding the notion of "hunter-gatherer" economies was far too simplistic. Indeed many peoples were really often cultivators, and their gathering grounds functioned as gardens. Through various methods, people encouraged the plants to grow, and looked after them. New ways of thinking about plant food production, as reflected in *Prehistoric Food Production in North America* (Ford 1985), have caused a re-evaluation of views on people's interrelationships with their lands, and this is true in the British Columbia interior.

Throughout the province, and especially in the interior, aboriginal people practised controlled burning to enhance the productivity and abundance of some of their plant resources, as well as for other purposes such as providing forage for deer and other game. They pruned berry bushes to make them more productive; they gathered plants selectively to maintain their populations; and they tilled, weeded and monitored patches of root vegetables. When harvesting them, they replanted smaller roots or portions of roots so they would continue growing. All of these processes were far from random. They represent a practical component of traditional ecological knowledge inextricably linked with spiritual and cultural foundations and respect for nature in all its forms. Together with effective methods for exchanging this knowledge, these processes comprise a complex knowledge system.

Since the first edition of this book was published, researchers have been paying more attention to the nutritional and health values of traditional foods. Research focusing on these values is still ongoing, but available evidence indicates that the traditional food systems of interior peoples, as of many other indigenous peoples, are very healthy. In many ways, people ate healthier food and lived healthier lifestyles than many of us in mainstream society do today.

The Preface to the First Edition names many people who contributed much to a better understanding and appreciation of traditional foods and philosophies surrounding their sustainable use in the British Columbia interior. Since the publication of the first edition, many others have contributed their knowledge in this field. Many of these people are acknowledged by name in *Traditional Plant Foods of Canadian Indigenous Peoples: Nutrition, Botany and Use* (Kuhnlein and Turner 1991), a book that incorporates the knowledge of indigenous elders and cultural experts across Canada, combined with nutritional analyses and research on traditional plant foods. I am particularly indebted to the following people (many of whom have passed away) for sharing their knowledge of plant foods with me in the years since the first edition was published: Mary Thomas, Nellie Taylor, Mary Palmantier, Lilly Harry and Aimee August (Secwepemc); Mabel Joe, Annie York, Hilda Austin and Louie Phillips (Nlaka'pamux); Sam Mitchell, Bill Edwards, Edith O'Donaghey, Desmond Peters Sr, Alec Peters, Nellie Peters and Margaret Lester (Stl'atl'imx); Helena Myers and Linda Smith (Tsilhqot'in); Julia and Charles Callbreath, and Sarah and Loveman Nole (Tahltan); and the elders of the Ulkatcho Nation who co-authored the newly published *Ulkatcho Food and Medicine Plants* (Hebda et al. 1996). Mary Sandy kindly shared the root foods from Washington shown in the photograph on page 82. Mary Thomas was particularly helpful in providing a number of the foods illustrated.

I would like to thank Gerry Truscott, Chief of Publishing Services at the Royal British Columbia Museum for his work in the production of this second edition. I also acknowledge my husband, Bob Turner, for his many photographs appearing in this edition, and the staff of the Royal B.C. Museum's herbarium for providing the photographs by W. van Dieren. Thanks also to Adolf Ceska for checking the scientific nomenclature and botanical descriptions in this edition, and to the staff of Royal B.C. Museum's anthropology section for helping to find the map on page 18 and for checking the spelling and pronunciation of First Nations names.

I am especially indebted to all those who are the knowledge keepers, whose recollections and detailed information enrich this book. Many of these people are named above and in the original preface. I hope that this new version of "the green book" (as some people called the first edition) will continue to be used as a reference guide, to raise the profile of these special plants and to emphasize their continuing importance to all British Columbians – especially to interior First Peoples, as integral components of their heritage and as persisting and profound constituents of their future lives.

Nancy J. Turner, Ph.D., FLS
School of Environmental Studies
University of Victoria
May 1997

An assortment of berries from the interior.

INTRODUCTION

Few British Columbians are aware of the abundance and variety of wild plant food to be found within the boundaries of their province. Some of the more common wild fruits, such as strawberries and Saskatoon Berries, are known to virtually everyone, but how many people know about the edibility of the hair-like Black Tree Lichen or the corms of the small herbaceous Spring Beauty, otherwise known as "Indian Potato"?

First Peoples in British Columbia used these and many other wild plants as important components of their diets. They learned, through careful observation and experimentation, the best seasons for gathering plant foods, the most efficient methods of harvesting them, the means of cooking and preparing them that best suited their taste and digestibility, and the ways of processing and storing them for year-round use.

This handbook and its companion, *Food Plants of Coastal First Peoples*, contain systematic accounts of plants used by British Columbian First Peoples as foods, flavourings and beverages, and for chewing and smoking. They include botanical descriptions of the plants, notations on their habitat and distribution in British Columbia, and information on their collection, preparation and use by aboriginal peoples.

These volumes have two purposes: to inform the public of the wide variety of edible plants in the province; and, for those interested in aboriginal history and culture, especially aboriginal people, to provide specific information on plants used by individual groups and the different methods employed for harvesting and preparing them. The books are designed primarily for use by non-professionals. I have avoided technical terminology as much as possible and supplemented the written botanical descriptions with photographs for easier identification of plants.

Many of the plants included in this book are common, and easy to recognize and gather. Others are cited only for completeness and academic interest, and are not recommended for consumption. All those wishing to sample wild plant foods should pay special attention to the notes concerning conservation and the potential of overharvesting native plants.

Berries, nuts and most types of greens can be gathered with little or no injury to the plants that bear them. But harvesting roots, bulbs, tubers and tree cambium can destroy individual plants and sometimes entire populations of a species – it should be practised only with the greatest discrimination.

For those inexperienced in plant identification, there is the ever-present danger of confusing an edible species with one that is inedible or even poisonous. A few wild plants in British Columbia can be fatal if consumed, even in small doses (some examples are Death Camas, Water Hemlock and False Hellebore); but many plants – even some considered edible at certain stages – can cause illness if eaten excessively or at the wrong time, or if prepared incorrectly. That you can eat the fruits or young shoots of a plant does not mean that the leaves, roots or older stems are also edible. There are many examples where quite the opposite is true.

Anyone interested in trying the aboriginal food plants described in this book should carefully consider the Warnings concerning the poisonous properties of some edible plants and the dangers of confusing edible with inedible species. It is also important to remember that these foods are still important to many First Nations. Would-be harvesters should respect private lands and traditional harvesting grounds when picking berries or gathering other food plants.

A new area of interest in traditional plant foods is their potential importance as non-timber forest products to enhance the economic value of standing forests. Many people now recognize that diversifying our use of forests is a component of sustainable forestry practices. Several bands and tribal councils in the interior have been investigating the marketing potential of traditional foods, as well as possibilities for commercial production of these foods for local and outside use.

Many people, too, are interested in growing native food plants as part of their home gardens, for their decorative value and food potential. This is an ecologically sound practice, since native plants are better adapted to the local climate and water regimes. They can also provide habitat and food for birds and other wildlife. Among several recent books on the propagation and growing of native plants, probably the best known and most complete is *Gardening with Native Plants of the Pacific Northwest* by Arthur Kruckeberg (1982), soon to be revised and republished.

Format

The plant descriptions in this book are arranged in an order that is partially botanical and partially practical. The major plant groups are in their traditional order: lichens, mushrooms and fungi, ferns, conifers, and flowering plants. (Algae and mosses were not used as food by British Columbia interior First Peoples, except for *Porphyra* seaweed, which some groups traded for.) The flowering plants are further divided into two subgroups: the monocotyledons and dicotyledons. The conifers, monocotyledons and dicotyledons are classed in families, which are presented in alphabetical order. Plants within a given family are listed alphabetically by scientific name, on the right-hand side of the page. The most commonly used English names of species and family appear at the left-hand side of the page. Alternate common names are also given where appropriate. Locally used names, which have restricted application and can sometimes be confusing, appear in quotation marks.

As might be expected, there is considerable overlap in the types of plants used as food by the coastal and interior First Peoples, although differences in culture and regional vegetation usually result in different emphasis placed on edible plants and in different methods of preparation. If a species is or was widely used by coastal and interior groups, it is included in the main text of both handbooks; but plants already discussed in the coastal handbook and used to a lesser extent by interior peoples are listed separately and without botanical descriptions in Appendix 1.

A number of species, while qualifying as food plants in a general sense, had only limited or sporadic use as sources of tea, tobacco, gum, casual edibles or flower nectar. For the sake of completeness these are included, without detail, in Appendix 2.

Appendix 3 contains some introduced and imported plant species that were important food sources to aboriginal peoples of the interior following contact with Europeans. Most are the same as those used during the same period by coastal First Peoples. Appendix 4 describes plants considered poisonous by people of one or more interior aboriginal groups.

Sources of Information

My major reference source for the botanical descriptions of the plants and details on their habitats and distributions was the five-volume work, *Vascular Plants of the Pacific Northwest* (Hitchcock et al. 1955-69). Many new botanical publications relating to the plants of British Columbia's interior have been written in the past two decades. Some of these are: *Trees and Shrubs of British Columbia* (Brayshaw 1996), as well as a number of monographic treatments of particular plant groups by T.C. Brayshaw; *Vascular Plants of British Columbia*, a four-volume set by Douglas et al. (1989-1994); *Trees, Shrubs and Flowers to Know in British Columbia and Washington* (Lyons and Merilees 1995); plant guides to northern British Columbia (MacKinnon et al. 1992), the southern interior (Parish et al. 1996) and the western boreal forest (Johnson et al. 1995); and *Ecosystems of British Columbia* (Meidinger and Pojar 1991). I have used some of these to update the botanical descriptions in this edition; others are mentioned for your interest.

I obtained information on the uses of food plants by the First Peoples of British Columbia's southern interior – the Stl'atl'imx, Nlaka'pamux, Okanagan, Secwepemc and Ktunaxa – in large part through interviews with the knowledgeable elders mentioned in the prefaces. I also consulted a number of publications, listed in References. Information on Tsilhqot'in, Ulkatcho Carrier, Gitxsan, Wet'suwet'en is from contemporary elders cited in more recent sources, some of which are mentioned below.

For the past six years I have been fortunate to work, together with Dr Marianne Ignace and many other Secwepemc and academic collaborators, on a major research project on Secwepemc Plant Knowledge. This research, undertaken through the Secwepemc Cultural Education Society and the Secwepemc Education Institute at Kamloops, has been funded by the Social Sciences and Humanities Research Council of Canada. One of the main goals of this project was to document the role of plants in traditional food systems of Secwepemc peoples. Ethnonutritionist Dr Harriet Kuhnlein, Director of the Centre for Indigenous Peoples' Nutrition and Environment (CINE) at McGill University, has been a key participant in this aspect of the project. Planned publications arising from this work will include substantial new information on the nutritional and cultural values of Secwepemc food plants.

Interior First Peoples' knowledge about and usage of plant foods are also described in a number of works that have been produced since the first edition of this book was published in 1978. Some important works are: "Conservation, territory and traditional beliefs" (Gottesfeld 1994c), *Gathering What the Great Nature Provided* ('Ksan 1980), "The role of plant foods in traditional Wet'suwet'en nutrition" (Gottesfeld 1995), "The importance of bark products in aboriginal economies of northwestern British Columbia" (Gottesfeld 1992), "Traditional foods of the Fraser Canyon Nlaka'pamux" (Laforet et al. 1993), *Ethnobotany of the Okanagan-Colville Indians of British Columbia and Washington* (Turner et al. 1980), *Thompson Ethnobotany* (Turner et al. 1990) and *Ulkatcho Plant Foods and Medicines* (Hebda et al. 1996), as well as Michèle Kay's master's thesis (1995) on Ulkatcho ethnobotany. Also relevant is a book on the ethnobotany of the Tanaina Athapaskan peoples of south-central Alaska, *Tanaina Plantlore: Dena'ina K'et'una* (Kari 1987). Other work on traditional food systems has been undertaken with interior peoples of Washington, such as *Nch'i-Wana. "The Big River." Mid-Columbia Indians and Their Land* (Hunn et al. 1990) and "Ethnobiology and subsistence" (Hunn et al. in press). Many papers and articles on specific topics relating to plant foods of interior peoples have also been published. I have listed many of these in References.

The use of plant foods by interior peoples of the past has also been a topic of increasing and ongoing interest among archaeologists and others. *Complex Cultures of the British Columbia Plateau: Traditional Stl'atl'imx Resource Use* (Hayden 1992) addresses some of the questions regarding plant usage by ancient peoples at Keatley Creek, above the Fraser River between Lillooet and Pavilion. Some other important works in archaeobotany, with information on traditional plant foods of the past, their harvesting and processing, are by David Pokotylo and Patricia Froese (1983), Diana Alexander and R.G. Matson (1987), Dana Lepofsky (1996), Sandra Peacock (in press) and their colleagues.

The Physical Environment

This handbook deals specifically with the interior First Peoples of British Columbia and the food plants growing in their territories. The total area is immense – the entire province east of the Cascade and Coast ranges.

Over such a large area, the physiography, climate and vegetation vary considerably, but we can still make generalizations about these features. Beginning in the west with the Coast and Cascade ranges, the British Columbia interior is dominated by a series of major mountain

Ponderosa Pine is the dominant tree, although Douglas-fir is common in cooler, moister areas.

The Interior Douglas-fir Zone is also dry, with a total annual precipitation of 36 to 56 cm. Besides Douglas-fir itself, some common trees of this zone are Ponderosa Pine, White Pine, Lodgepole Pine, Western Larch, Trembling Aspen, Black Cottonwood, Rocky Mountain Maple, and Paper Birch.

The Montane Spruce Zone is characterized by Engelmann and hybrid spruce, as well as some Subalpine Fir. Due to past fires, successional forests of Lodgepole Pine, Douglas-fir and Trembling Aspen dominate the landscape. This zone borders the upper limits of the Interior Douglas-fir Zone.

The Interior Cedar - Hemlock Zone occurs in lower and middle elevations in the interior wet belt and in the Skeena and Nass river valleys in the northwest. Cool, wet winters and warm, dry summers make this zone the most productive in the interior, producing the widest variety of coniferous trees. Western Red-cedar and Western Hemlock are characteristic, but spruces and Subalpine Fir are also common, as well as Douglas-fir and Lodgepole Pine in the drier areas.

One of the wettest zones in the interior is the Engelmann Spruce - Subalpine Fir Zone, a montane zone with an annual precipitation of 41 to 183 cm, most of it in the form of snow. Common trees in this zone, besides Engelmann Spruce and Subalpine Fir, are Lodgepole Pine, Whitebark Pine and Alpine Larch. All of these species tolerate harsh winters with extended periods of frozen ground.

The Sub-boreal Spruce Zone is in the central interior, mostly on plateaus. It is an intermediate zone between the southern Douglas-fir forests and northern boreal forests. The dominant trees are hybrid Engelmann-White Spruce and Subalpine Fir. Wetlands in poorly drained areas are common here.

The Sub-boreal Pine - Spruce Zone is on the high plateau of the central interior in the rain-shadow of the Coast Mountains. The cold, dry climate and long winters make this zone low in productivity. Extensive forest fires have encouraged the growth of Lodgepole Pine in many areas, and some White Spruce also grows here. Pinegrass and Kinnikinnick are common in the understorey.

The Boreal White and Black Spruce Zone is part of the belt of boreal coniferous forest that stretches across northern Canada. In British Columbia it occupies the Great Plains east of the Rocky Mountains and river valleys in the northwest. Long, cold winters and the short growing season make for poor plant growth. Black Spruce bogs and stands of White Spruce and Trembling Aspen are common.

The Spruce - Willow - Birch Zone occupies the subalpine areas in the north. The climate is severe: upper elevations are dominated by shrubs and scrub birch and willow, and lower elevations by open forests of White Spruce and Subalpine Fir.

Finally, the Alpine Tundra Zone occurs throughout the province above the timberline. Conditions on the high mountains are too severe for woody plants, except in dwarf forms. The vegetation is dominated by herbs, mosses, lichens and some dwarf shrubs. Aboriginal peoples occasionally ventured into it for hunting and some plant gathering.

You can learn more about these zones and their vegetation from the Ministry of Forests' wall map, *Biogeoclimatic Zones of British Columbia* (1992) and *Ecosystems of British Columbia* (Meidinger and Pojar 1991). Many of the edible plant species mentioned in this book are restricted to one or two of these zones, or are more abundant and productive in some than others. Hence, the types and quantities of plant foods available to different aboriginal groups throughout the interior vary substantially. In the past, aboriginal peoples often reduced their resource deficiencies by trading. A number of plants with limited natural ranges, such as Bitter-root, Hazelnut and Dwarf Blueberry, reached more people through trade. But even the widespread exchange of produce could not correct the lower diversity of plant resources in some areas. The Athapaskan peoples of the northern biogeoclimatic zones generally had fewer types of wild plant foods available to them and hence their aboriginal diet contained a higher proportion of animal products. The other zones yield a greater diversity and abundance of edible plants, providing a rich vegetable diet to the aboriginal peoples who had access to them.

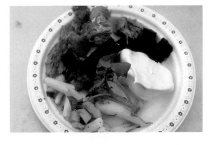

Traditional Secwepemc foods, clockwise from top: salmon, Moose, Black Tree Lichen, whipped Soapberries, Watercress and Yellow Avalanche Lily bulbs.

First Peoples of the Interior

In this book, I have distinguished the aboriginal groups of British Columbia's interior by the languages they speak. The table on the facing page shows the name of each language group, its general pronunciation and its former or alternate name, where applicable. There are differences in the ways individual First Peoples say these names, so the pronunciations are approximations at best. The territories occupied by these groups are shown on the map on page 18.

The Athapaskan family of languages also includes Navaho and Apache of the southwestern United States. Before contact with Europeans, a group of Athapaskan peoples occupied an area in southern British Columbia around the Nicola and Similkameen rivers, but they have since been assimilated into their Salish neighbours. The region is now inhabited by Nlaka'pamux and Okanagan peoples. Inland Tlingit is related to coastal Tlingit of Alaska, and as such distantly related to Athapaskan languages. Ktunaxa is considered a linguistic isolate, not known to be closely related to any other language. You can obtain further information on the languages and cultural characteristics of these peoples from the Smithsonian handbook on Plateau cultures (Walker in press).

Interior First Peoples belong to two culture areas – the Sub-Arctic and the Plateau – and some language groups are transitional with adjacent culture areas. The Sub-Arctic Culture Area comprises the various Athapaskan groups of central and northern British Columbia, along with the peoples of central Alaska, the Yukon, the western Northwest Territories, and northern Alberta and Saskatchewan. The peoples of this culture area traditionally lived in widely scattered communities, and they travelled in birch-bark and spruce-bark canoes or on snowshoes. They depended – and still depend – heavily on the meat of large game animals such as Moose and Caribou for food. They did not use plant foods as extensively as groups in the south, but they still used several species of berries, tree cambium, and a few types of edible roots and greens.

The Plateau Culture Area includes the Salishan peoples of the Interior Plateau (Interior Salish) and the Ktunaxa people of eastern British Columbia together with the various Salishan peoples and the Nez Perce and Sahaptin of Washington, Oregon, Idaho and western Montana. (The Lakes people, mentioned specifically in this book, speak a subdialect of Northern Okanagan.) These groups, especially the Ktunaxa, possessed some of the cultural traits of the Plains peoples,

First Nations of British Columbia

Language Family People Dialect	General Pronunciation*	Former or Alternative Name
Interior Groups		
Interior Salish	Say-lish	
Stl'atl'imx	Stlat-liem*x*	Lillooet
Upper		Fraser River
Lower		Lil'wat
Okanagan	O-kan-aw-gan	Okanagan-Colville
Northern Okanagan		
Southern Okanagan		
Secwepemc	Se-wep-m*x*	Shuswap
Nlaka'pamux	Ng-khla-kap-muh*x*	Thompson
Upper		
Lower		
Kalispel [Washington]	Kal-i-spell	
Ktunaxa	Doon-ah-hah	Kootenay, Kutenai
Athapaskan		
Tsilhqot'in	Tsil-ko-teen	Chilcotin
Carrier (Dakelh)	(Da-kelh)	
Ulkatcho	Ul-gat-cho	Carrier
Cree	Kree	
Wet'suwet'en	Wet-so-wet-en	Babine Carrier
Sekani	Sik-an-ee	
Dunne-za	De-nay-za	Beaver
Dene-thah	De-nay-ta	Slave(y)
Tahltan	Tall-ten	
Kaska	Kas-ka	
Tagish	Ta-gish	
Tlingit	Tling-git	
Inland Tlingit		
Tsimshian	Sim-she-an	
Nisga'a	Nis-ga-a	Nishga
Gitxsan	Git-ksan	Tsimshian
Coastal Groups		
Haida	Hydah	
Wakashan	Wokashan	
Haisla	Hyzlah	Kitimat
Heiltsuk	Heel-tsuk	Bella Bella
Oweekeno	O-wik-en-o	Kwakiutl
Kwakwaka'wakw	Kwok-wok-ee-wok	Kwakiutl, Kwagiulth
Nuu-chah-nulth	New-cha-nulth	Nootka
Coast Salish	Coast Say-lish	
Nuxalk	New-halk	Bella Coola
Comox	Ko-moks	
Sechelt	Seeshelt	
Squamish	Skwamish	
Halkomelem	Halk-o-may-lem	
Straits Salish	Straits Say-lish	

---

* The pronunciations are approximations. Note that the italic*x* in the pronunciation column designates the fricative sound similar to the German *ich.*

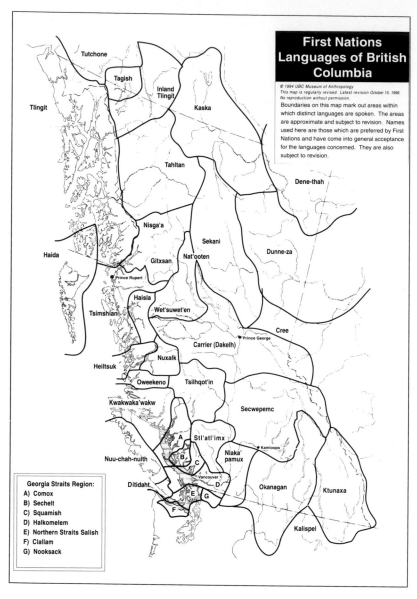

First Nations Languages of British Columbia

© 1994 UBC Museum of Anthropology
This map is regularly revised. Latest revision October 15, 1996.
No reproduction without permission.
Boundaries on this map mark out areas within which distinct languages are spoken. The areas are approximate and subject to revision. Names used here are those which are preferred by First Nations and have come into general acceptance for the languages concerned. They are also subject to revision.

Tutchone

Tagish

Inland Tlingit

Tlingit

Kaska

Tahltan

Dene-thah

Nisga'a

Sekani

Haida

Gitxsan

Nat'ooten

Dunne-za

Prince Rupert

Haisla

Tsimshian

Wet'suwet'en

Cree

Carrier (Dakelh)

Prince George

Heiltsuk

Nuxalk

Oweekeno

Tsilhqot'in

Kwakwaka'wakw

Secwepemc

A

Stl'atl'imx

Kamloops

B

Nlaka'pamux

C

Nuu-chah-nulth

Vancouver

D

Ditidaht

E

G

Okanagan

Ktunaxa

F

Kalispel

Georgia Straits Region:
A) Comox
B) Sechelt
C) Squamish
D) Halkomelem
E) Northern Straits Salish
F) Clallam
G) Nooksack

The boundaries of territories on this map are approximate. In most cases, the people are named for the language they speak; but Kwakwaka'wakw is the name of the people who speak the Kwakwala language. For consistency in this book, I have used the name of the people rather than the language on this map.

but were generally more sedentary. The Plateau peoples depend heavily on Pacific salmon, which still come in great numbers every year up the Fraser and Columbia rivers to their spawning streams (though the populations have declined significantly since Europeans arrived). Plateau peoples used a great variety of plant foods, especially berries and edible roots and bulbs, and some people still use large quantities of these foods.

The Inland Tlingit, Nisga'a, Gitxsan, Ulkatcho, Lower Stl'atl'imx (Lil'wat) and Lower Nlaka'pamux are all on the border of the Northwest Coast Culture Area and share many cultural features with groups of the coast. They had access to a number of coastal plant foods not readily available to other interior groups, but were also able to use some interior foods not accessible to coastal peoples.

Although each group uses plant foods in different ways, particularly in their methods of harvesting and preparing them, many use the same species and employ similar methods of processing, such as dehydrating berries and cooking in earth ovens or underground pits. Cree foods are not discussed in this book; for information on Cree knowledge and use of plant foods, consult Leighton (1985), listed in References.

Plants in the Diets of Interior First Peoples

The major types of plant foods used by interior First Peoples are fruits (berries, nuts and seeds), green vegetables (sprouts and leaves), tree lichen (one kind only), mushrooms, underground parts (roots, bulbs, rhizomes, corms and tubers), and cambium, inner bark, sweet sap and sugar from certain trees. Many berries, some mushrooms, and certain greens and underground parts are still harvested today, and some are increasingly important as the nutritional and health advantages of traditional foods are rediscovered.

Plant products contributed only a portion of the total food intake of most interior aboriginal peoples, especially those in central and northern British Columbia. But plant foods were more significant in the southern areas – a recent study estimates their caloric contribution to the total diet at 50 per cent or more (see Hunn et al. in press).

Foods containing carbohydrates, so scarce on the coast, were considerably more plentiful in the southern interior. There, aboriginal peoples used a wide variety of underground parts containing carbohydrates, as well as some seeds and nuts, and Black Tree Lichen. According to Yanovsky and Kingsbury (1938), the lichen has a substantial carbohydrate content. The peoples of the northern interior, on the other hand, must have consumed even fewer carbohydrates than the coastal First Peoples, judging from ethnographic reports. There, as on the coast and in the Arctic, the caloric contribution of carbohydrates was replaced largely by animal fats and oils. In this regard, the peoples of the northern interior were further deprived in not having easy access to Eulachon grease and other fish oils so valuable to their coastal counterparts; instead they used deer fat, bear grease and other animal fats.

As on the coast, when carbohydrates in the form of flour, rice, potatoes, turnips, carrots and beans were introduced by Europeans, they attained immediate popularity with the interior aboriginal people, even those of the southern part of the province.

Vegetable protein was in short supply, but this shortage was amply compensated for by the abundance of animal protein. Interior First Peoples ate fish or meat with almost every vegetable dish. Green vegetables, such as the sprouts of Cow Parsnip, Balsamroot, prickly-pear cactus, "Indian Celery" and Fireweed, and the nutrient-rich cambium and inner bark of Lodgepole Pine and other trees provided vitamins and minerals, as well as dietary fibre.

Of course, aboriginal peoples had no knowledge of refined sugar until the coming of Europeans, and as such, did not have any of the candies and confections we consume so much of today. When sugar was introduced, it was eagerly sought, and used in large quantities. Nevertheless, even before this time, a number of wild plants yielded special confections that people ate as desserts and treats. Most notable among these was Indian ice cream*, made by whipping the bitter-tasting berries of the Soapberry with water into a frothy mixture resembling beaten egg-white. Indian ice cream was relished by all aboriginal peoples in the province, coast and interior alike. Many people still eat it, although now they sweeten it with sugar instead of Saskatoons or other berries as their grandparents did.

Interior peoples often treated Saskatoon Berries, by themselves, as a dessert. Some varieties of this fruit were more popular than others, being considered sweeter and of better flavour. Some types were dried individually and eaten like raisins, while others were mashed and dried in cakes, which could be cut up later and given to children as candy bars, or rehydrated and mixed with other ingredients to make a pud-

---

*This is not the Indian ice cream of some Tsimshian people and other northern groups, which is made by collecting the second fall of snow and mixing it with grease or fat, berries and (nowadays) sugar. The result looks and tastes very similar to commercial ice cream.

ding. Other dried berries also made popular treats. Secwepemc elder Mary Thomas recalled a wonderful treat her grandmother made from dried strawberries, raspberries or Thimbleberries. The outside was firm, but the inside was like jelly. Children loved it.

Certain roots, especially Balsamroot, Yellow Avalanche Lily and Bitter-root, were often considered as dessert foods, and were cooked and eaten after a main course as a special treat. Today, these foods are sometimes incorporated into modern desserts (see for example, the recipe for Bitter-root pudding on page 138).

An unusual confection, only occasionally available in certain areas of the southern interior, was a type of sugar that sometimes crystallizes on the needles and branches of the interior variety of Douglas-fir. This hard, white substance is completely soluble in water and is perhaps the world's most highly concentrated source of a rare trisaccharide sugar known as melezitose. It was eagerly sought after by Interior Salish peoples, but was regarded as an extra rather than a necessary part of the diet, because its occurrence is so sporadic. This sugar is discussed in greater detail in the account for Douglas-fir in the main text. Another sweet enjoyed by the Ktunaxa people and the Flathead of Montana was a liquid syrup collected from certain trees of Western Larch.

Interior First Peoples employed a number of plants to make non-medicinal beverages and smoking mixtures. The important species used for this purpose, or used as food in some other way, are included

Stl'atl'imx woman making baskets, 1902. (RBCM PN6632)

A woman and child digging up roots in upper Botanie Valley (from Davidson 1915).

in the main text; less important species used solely for smoking or making beverages are listed in Appendix 2. The most widely used tea plants are Labrador Tea and Trapper's Tea, and the most common tobacco was Kinnikinnick.

Harvesting Food Plants

Interior First Peoples, like their coastal counterparts and many other peoples throughout the world, practised a division of labour in their quest for subsistence, such that the harvesting of vegetable foods was mainly the responsibility of the women, whereas hunting and fishing were carried out by the men. Cooking and preparation of the food for winter storage was undertaken by both men and women, but mainly by women.

Collecting a year's supply of fruits and vegetables for a family was hard and serious work, but not without its pleasures, as anyone who has

Botanie Valley: an important resource area and gathering place.

spent a day picking berries will appreciate. Harvesting was usually a group activity and was thus a social occasion as well as one of labour. Imagine what it must have been like: women, old and young alike, busily stripping fruit-laden bushes or prying roots out of the ground, deftly cleaning the roots and tossing them into baskets, the younger ones laughing and chattering and the grandmothers giving advice, with the sounds of children playing nearby.

Some of the larger berry-picking and root-digging grounds, such as Botanie Valley, north of Lytton, near the junction of the Fraser and Thompson rivers, actually became centres for large-scale, inter-tribal exchange. Every year in late spring, when the "Indian Potato", Yellow Avalanche Lily and other roots were ready to be dug, families gathered at Botanie Valley from all over the surrounding countryside to partake in the harvest. Nlaka'pamux, Stl'atl'imx and even Secwepemc peoples converged there; the Nlaka'pamux acted as hosts, since they owned the valley. The valley assumed the atmosphere of a country fair, with games and competitions, reunions of old friends and relatives, and the courting of sweethearts.

Louie Phillips, of the Nlaka'pamux Nation at Lytton, recalled that in his boyhood, horse-racing was a popular sport at Botanie. Adding a modern twist to the occupation of root-digging, the women would climb the steep slopes of the valley to dig up Yellow Avalanche Lily bulbs on the ridge tops, at the same time gaining an excellent view of the racing on the valley floor below. Each woman picked her favourite horse and, to introduce an element of risk to her labours, would bet half, or even her entire day's harvest on the horses of her choice. At the end of the day, some women returned empty-handed, despite having worked hard, and others, on whom fortune had smiled, staggered down with huge gunny-sacks full of roots. These carefree days are gone, but people still go to Botanie Valley to harvest "Indian Potatoes", "Indian Celery" and other traditional plants.

Berry patches and root-digging areas in the interior could be owned by chiefs or families, just as they were on the coast, but many areas were held as common tribal property. A chief often controlled and supervised the harvest, especially in areas where the berries or roots were likely to be in short supply. No one could pick berries or dig roots without direction and advice of the chief or a designated elder as to which patches were ready for harvest at any given time. This method ensured maximum efficiency of harvesting, to the benefit of the entire village.

Sometimes, aboriginal groups honoured the spirits of important berries and roots with a First Fruits or First Roots ceremony, thus ensuring a good harvest for the present and succeeding years. The Okanagan at Penticton held a First Roots ceremony for Bitter-root, designated by some as the chief of all the roots. They often honoured Saskatoon Berries in this way also.

Traditional Bitter-root digging grounds of the Penticton people are in two high flatlands locally known as Pierre and Roddy flats, west of Penticton. Each year in May when the Bitter-root flower buds appeared, the chief and elders selected four of the purest young women to dig the first roots, four other women to pick the first Saskatoon Berries and four young men to go hunting and fishing. When these first harvesters had collected enough roots, berries and game, the entire village celebrated with a large feast to thank the foods for returning once more for the benefit of the people. After this feast, anyone in the village could go out to get Bitter-root or Saskatoons*.

Equipment for harvesting plant foods was simple but practical. Aboriginal harvesters picked most berries by hand, except for a few species of low blueberry, such as Dwarf Blueberry and Grouseberry. These they raked off the bushes with long-toothed combs, because the berries were too small and close to the ground to pick up with the fingers. People gathered Soapberries by placing mats, buckets or trays beneath the bushes and whacking the branches sharply with a stick, so that the ripe berries fell onto the mats or into the containers.

Many interior peoples dug roots with an ingenious tool known as a pátsa (pronounced "pa´cha") in Stl'atl'imx and Secwepemc or pítsa (pronounced "pee´cha") in Okanagan. Ranging in length from about

---

*This information was related by Selina Timoyakin of the Penticton Band, who recalled these events from her girlhood.

30 to 120 cm, it had a curved, pointed tip and a short crosspiece handle at the top. People once made digging-sticks of hard wood, such as Oceanspray, Black Hawthorn or Saskatoon Berry, or of Mule Deer or Elk antler, but nowadays they often use an iron bar with a metal or wooden handle. Even today, many aboriginal people own digging-sticks. They are far more efficient than a shovel for harvesting wild roots and bulbs, as long as the ground is soft and loamy.

Secwepemc digging stick, made of Black Hawthorn.

To harvest tree cambium, interior First Peoples used a sharp bone scraper or, more recently, a thin piece of curved metal, sometimes cut from a tin can.

Containers for harvesting berries and roots, as well as for cooking and transport, included tightly woven coiled baskets of split cedar root, bark containers of birch or White Spruce, and strong fibre bags of Tule, Indian Hemp, and the bark of Silverberry or Sandbar Willow.

The Interior Salish specialized in making the cedar-root baskets, many with beautiful decorative overlays made with wild cherry bark and grass stems (such as Reed Canary Grass or Giant Wild-rye). A good basket maker could produce a water-tight container, suitable even for boiling food with hot rocks. Athapaskan and Ktunaxa peoples, and also the eastern Secwepemc and some Okanagan people, were experts in the art of making birch-bark baskets. These are also water-tight when

The late Sam Mitchell digging up Spring Beauty roots at Pavilion Mountain.

Hazelnuts gathered in a basket.

made properly, and are beautiful as well as sturdy. Spruce-bark baskets were made in the same style as those of birch bark, but were not as well finished, and were usually only for temporary use. Berry pickers often slung these baskets over the shoulders or around the neck or forehead with a tumpline, or tied them around the waist to leave the hands free.

Some groups, mainly in the Salish area, employed fibre bags for harvesting and storing roots. Later, they replaced fibre bags with gunnysacks, flour sacks and canvas bags. Aboriginal peoples in the regions bordering the coastal zone traded for containers of the coastal type – cedar-bark and spruce-root baskets and cedar cooking boxes.

Unfortunately, these beautiful yet practical artifacts have almost entirely given way to metal pans and buckets, and to those wonders of modern technology, the plastic bag and the ice-cream bucket. Basketmaking arts live on in some communities, thanks to the skill and dedication of people such as Margaret Lester, Nellie Peters and Mary Thomas.

Preparing Food Plants

Some plant foods, such as green sprouts, some roots and a few juicy types of berries, could be eaten just as they were harvested, without cooking or preparation. But most had to be cooked, if they were to be eaten immediately, or prepared for storage so they would not rot or spoil, if they were to be kept for use at some later time. Preparation and cooking procedures varied among different groups and each type of food was treated in a different way. Here are a few examples of different procedures:

Berry pickers, after de-stemming and sorting their fruits, could dry them by any one of several methods. Some berries, such as certain varieties of Saskatoon, they would spread out and dry like raisins. Other types they would cook, mash and spread out on layers of branches and grass or woven mats to dry as cakes. Some people might light a fire nearby or underneath a frame of berries. They would rarely lay berries under direct sunlight; the warm summer air was usually sufficient to dehydrate them within a few days. People often collected the juice from berries as they cooked, and later poured it over the drying berry cakes a little at a time; the juice solidified, giving the finished product a jelly-like consistency. People used this method for preserving Saskatoons, raspberries, Soapberries and blueberries, among others. Sometimes, people dried berries in cakes without cooking them, by merely mashing and spreading them out over grass, pine needles or mats for several days.

People ate dried berries and berry cakes at any time without rehydrating, or they soaked them in water overnight to reconstitute them. Many elders recall that people often mixed sweet berries with sour or bitter ones: an equal measure of Saskatoon Berries made Red-Osier Dogwood berries much more palatable. They did this with fresh berries and reconstituted berry cakes. They also mixed berries with other foods, including salmon eggs and Bitter-root, and nowadays use them as ingredients in puddings, muffins and fruit cakes.

People used to store some roots and underground parts fresh, after digging, peeling and cleaning them. They buried the roots in underground pits, a metre or more deep, and kept them for several months like this. They lined the pits with pine needles and covered them with a thick layer of earth to protect the roots from the frost. Sometimes they packed their caches of roots with large slabs of Black Cottonwood bark to keep out ground squirrels and other burrowing rodents. "Indian Potatoes", Wild Caraway roots and a variety of other roots, as well as dried berries, dried meat, and dried fish, could be stored by this method. People also constructed above-ground caches in trees and on raised posts for short-term storage of such foods.

Some peoples, such as the Secwepemc and Carrier, threaded Yellow Avalanche Lily bulbs and other roots onto long strings, which they hung up to dry. G. Palmer in "Shuswap Indian Ethnobotany" (1975) notes that the Secwepemc in the late nineteenth century valued a string of dried Yellow Avalanche Lily bulbs tied in a circular string about a metre in diameter at five dollars. People rarely dried Bitter-roots on strings but usually spread them out in the sun. Sometimes they used thin skewers to dry these and other roots. Dried roots could be reconstituted by boiling or steaming them.

Most people cooked roots and underground parts in steaming pits, similar to those used by coastal First Peoples. To make a steaming pit, they dug a hole knee to waist deep and wide enough to accommodate the quantity of food to be cooked, and lined it with large, round rocks. They lit a fire in the bottom of the pit to heat the rocks red-hot; sometimes they heated the rocks in a fire beside the pit. Then they dispersed the coals and placed soil, grass, branches and leaves over the rocks. They spread a layer of roots or bulbs over this material and covered them with another layer of vegetation. Sometimes they put the food in bags or on woven trays to protect it from dirt and ashes. Then they covered the pit with earth, and usually kindled another fire on top. To generate more steam in the pit, they could add water through a small hole; they had made the hole by holding an upright stick in the pit as they filled it. Pulling out the stick, they could pour water down the hole to the hot rocks at the bottom. Then they plugged the opening and left the food to cook for several hours or overnight. There are many variations of this process.

Pit-steaming (called "barbecuing" by some people) was used to cook such foods as Balsamroot, wild onions, Chocolate Lily bulbs and "Indian Potatoes". Pit-ovens can retain heat near the boiling point for several hours before gradually cooling. They are an effective and efficient method for cooking large quantities of roots and other foods.

People also cooked roots and bulbs by boiling them in baskets or, more recently, in kettles and pots. They often cooked them together with fish or meat in a kind of stew, or in other nutritious combinations of plant and animal foods.

Black Tree Lichen, widely used in the interior, especially as an emergency food, had to be soaked and steam-cooked before it was fit to eat. People commonly steamed it in a pit with layers of wild onions or other foods to add flavour. After cooking it, they ate it immediately or cut it into loaves and dried it for winter.

Many people enjoyed the cambium and inner bark tissues of Lodgepole Pine and other trees, usually eating it fresh, but sometimes drying it in cakes for later use. Some kinds of mushrooms were also eaten; people cooked them and either ate them fresh or dried them in strings. Seeds and nuts were simply stored in a cool, dry place until needed.

Today these methods of cooking and preparing plant foods have given way almost entirely to modern techniques. People usually steam foods in steamers or pressure cookers rather than pit-ovens. They seldom preserve foods by drying them, but when they do they often use an oven or food dehydrator. They preserve most fruits by canning, freezing or making jam; they even can or freeze mushrooms. Still, many old-timers maintain that the foods taste best when cooked in the time-honoured ways of the past.

Food Plants Throughout the Seasons

Winters throughout British Columbia's interior are long and severe. In the south, the growing season begins in March or April, much later at higher elevations. The appearance of the first shoots of greenery each year marked, for aboriginal peoples, the beginning of the quest for vegetable foods, which would continue until the snowfalls of the following winter.

At the beginning of the growing season, people eagerly sought newly sprouted greens. After the winter's fare of dried food, which may have been in short supply by the end of winter, greens were especially appreciated. As early as March, harvesting parties ventured out in search of Balsamroot shoots. Though the shoots had not yet appeared above ground, the harvesters located them by their proximity to the previous year's flowering-stalks. They dug up the shoots and ate them fresh. They also ate the sprouts of Chocolate Tips, though they considered the mature stems poisonous. Later, in April and May, other greens were ready for harvesting, including Cow Parsnip and Fireweed stalks, and "Indian Celery" leaves.

Also at this time, various roots were ready for digging. Harvesting the bulbs of Yellowbell, Chocolate Lily, Mariposa Lily and Nodding Onions began in April and continued to early May, before the plants flowered. Balsamroot, Bitter-root and "Wild Carrots" were also ready to harvest at that time. In late May and June, people gathered "Indian Potatoes" from the upland meadows, and also Tiger Lily bulbs and Wild Caraway. They dug Yellow Avalanche Lily bulbs from late May until the end of summer, depending on the elevation at which the plants were growing, but usually after the leaves turned yellow.

In the Okanagan Valley, Ponderosa Pine cambium was at the right stage for collecting in mid May; Lodgepole Pine, found at higher elevations, was ready about three weeks later. In June the early varieties of Saskatoon Berries were ready for picking, as were the wild strawberries. By July, different species of berries were ripening in quick succession, beginning with Saskatoon Berries and Soapberries, followed by wild raspberries, Blackcaps, low-elevation blueberries, Black Hawthorn berries, Thimbleberries, Red-Osier Dogwood berries, and wild gooseberries and currants. Toward late summer the berries of the upper elevations, such as Mountain Blueberries and huckleberries, began to ripen, as did Whitebark Pine seeds. The women made frequent trips into the mountains at this time to gather them, and also to pick Black Tree Lichen, although lichen could be collected at any time during the summer or fall. At lower elevations, Hazelnuts and Blue Elderberries ripened in late summer.

Finally, in the fall, mushrooms grew and such fruits as Bog Cranberries, High-bush Cranberries, wild rose hips, Crowberries and Kinnikinnick berries were ready to be gathered. These berries could be harvested even after a heavy frost – freezing actually makes them softer and sweeter. They were the only fruits that could still be found on the bushes in mid winter in times of emergency.

By the end of fall, each family would not only have enjoyed many meals of fresh produce but also would have preserved and stored enough fruits and vegetables for use throughout the winter. An interior Salish family's winter store might include 100 kg of Yellow Avalanche Lily bulbs, dried Bitter-roots and other roots, 50 kg or more of dried Saskatoon Berries, as well as dried cakes of Soapberries, blueberries, raspberries, and Red-Osier Dogwood, Black Hawthorn and other berries, a large supply of dried Black Tree Lichen, many strings of dried mushrooms, and several sacks of Balsamroot seeds, Hazelnuts or Whitebark Pine nuts. These and a winter supply of dried salmon, salmon oils and animal fat, deer meat, and other animal foods permitted the family a comfortable existence during the cold season – their absence made survival nearly impossible.

Trading Food Plants

For centuries the First Peoples of British Columbia and adjacent regions have traded materials and produce. Trading allowed for a more even distribution of the land's resources, giving every group access to a greater variety of foods and raw materials than their own territories provided; it also afforded opportunities for social interchange. The interior First Peoples maintained a number of well-used trade routes through the Cascade and Coast mountains to the coast, mostly along the major river valleys, such as the Fraser, Lillooet, Bella Coola, Nass,

Skeena and Stikine. They also had many trade routes throughout the interior.

An example of a coast-interior trading arrangement was between the Lower Stl'atl'imx (Lil'wat) of the Pemberton area and the Halkomelem peoples of the Fraser River valley. The Stl'atl'imx made yearly journeys to the Fraser River valley via the Lillooet River and Harrison Lake to obtain such coastal goods as dentalia shells, cedar bark, Pacific Yew, Vine Maple and Yellow-cedar wood, Hazelnuts, dried huckleberries, goat-hair blankets and fish oil. In exchange, they brought interior products such as Indian Hemp, willow-bark twine, dried and strung Yellow Avalanche Lily bulbs, dried Saskatoons, Soapberries, Choke Cherries, dried meat, fat and animal skins. The Lower Nlaka'pamux and Halkomelem had a similar arrangement, as did the Lower Stl'atl'imx and Sechelt. Further north, the Ulkatcho and Tsilhqot'in traded Yellow Avalanche Lily bulbs, blueberries and Soapberries, among other items, with the Nuxalk for dried seaweed, Wild Crabapples, High-bush Cranberries, Western Red-cedar products, salmon and Eulachon grease. The Gitxsan, Nisga'a, Wet'suwet'en, Tahltan and Inland Tlingit also exchanged comparable goods with their coastal counterparts.

Nevertheless, aboriginal groups of the interior traded among themselves far more often than with coastal groups. Plant foods involved in such exchanges included Bitter-roots, Yellow Avalanche Lily bulbs, "Indian Potatoes", "Indian Carrots", Blue Camas bulbs, dried Saskatoons, Soapberries, currants, blueberries and Labrador Tea. Sometimes these foods were bought and sold fully processed, while other times, arrangements were made for neighbouring groups to come and harvest the produce themselves – a classic example of the "pick your own" tradition. The importance of Botanie Valley as an area for such commercial activities has already been mentioned.

After the coming of Europeans and the introduction of a wide variety of new trade products, including plant foods such as potatoes, carrots, beans, onions, raisins, rice, flour and sugar, trading increased in volume and complexity, until most items became available in stores and many indigenous plant foods gave way almost entirely to commercial and garden-grown vegetables and fruits. Today, interior First Peoples still use wild produce and consider it a high-value commodity. Among the best gifts to receive are wild berry jams, dried or frozen root vegetables, wild mushrooms and jarred Soapberry concentrate for juice or whipping into Indian ice cream.

LICHENS
(Lichenes)

Black Tree Lichen
(Alectoria Family)

Bryoria fremontii Tuck.
(Alectoriaceae)

Other Names: "Black Tree Moss", "Edible Lichen", "Indian Bread".

Botanical Description
Black Tree Lichen is a long, hair-like lichen, dark-brown to black. It hangs from the branches of trees; in good locations, it can attain a length of 60 to 90 cm. When dry, its texture is like steel wool; when wet, it is soft and limp. The lichen's branches are long, round to flattened and smooth; they hang in tangled masses. Sometimes the branches bear greenish or sulphur-coloured powdery fragments called soredia. The fruiting discs, when present, are small (2 to 6 mm across) and yellow. *Bryoria fremontii* is in a general complex, *Alectoria jubata*, which is an archaic grouping of several similar species.

Habitat: tree branches, mainly of coniferous species such as Ponderosa Pine, Douglas-fir and Western Larch; most prevalent in upper branches and on north-facing slopes; commonly grows with Wolf Lichen, which is wiry, yellow-green and inedible.

Distribution in British Columbia: throughout the interior, especially in montane forests.

Aboriginal Use
Black Tree Lichen (and possibly some of its relatives) was used as a food by virtually every aboriginal group in the interior, but was not used on the coast, according to available information. It apparently has an un-

Black Tree Lichen prepared for pit cooking (left) and made into loaves (right). See page 50 for a photograph of Black Tree Lichen hanging from the branches of a Western Larch.

usually low concentration of a bitter-tasting compound known as vulpinic acid, which renders closely related species inedible and even poisonous. Even so, it usually had to be specially treated before people considered it fit to eat.

Opinions vary widely as to its quality as a food. Some aboriginal people say that, prepared properly, it is delicious, "like candy", whereas others feel it is an inferior food, to be eaten only in times of emergency when other foods are not available. This discrepancy may be due to varied concentrations of vulpinic acid and other lichen substances in local populations of Black Tree Lichen, or to the use of other species of *Bryoria*. Some people maintain that the only way to tell if the lichen is good or bad is to taste a sample before it is harvested. In the Okanagan area, for example, young hunters would collect small pieces of it from certain mountain slopes and bring them back for their grandmothers or mothers to taste. If it was "sweet" rather than bitter, the family would claim the area where it was growing and collect the lichen from the trees in the vicinity.

"Black Tree Moss" can be gathered at any time of the year; some groups collected it in June, others in the fall after all the other foods had been harvested. Its flavour is affected by the type of tree it is growing on. The Northern Okanagan and Secwepemc preferred it when growing on Ponderosa Pine or Lodgepole Pine; some Stl'atl'imx and Southern Okanagan people believed it to be best from Douglas-fir or Western Larch, saying it had an unpleasant pitchy flavour if taken from pines. People used long poles to pull the lichen from the branches or sent youngsters to climb the trees and gather it by hand; sometimes they would cut the entire tree down. In a good location, five or six trees would yield a sufficient harvest for one family for the year.

The fresh lichen is light, but bulky. Harvesters packed it into large sacks or tied it in bales, which they carried or rolled down to the camp. In an emergency, Black Tree Lichen could be eaten raw, but it is often bitter and may colour the saliva green. Interior people usually prepared it by removing any twigs or dirt that might be entangled in it, then soaking it in fresh water to remove the bitterness, and finally steaming it overnight or longer in a pit lined with bunchgrass or other vegetation (described in the introductory section, Preparation of Food Plants) until it had attained the consistency of stringy fresh dough and the appearance of licorice. Black Tree Lichen compacts with cooking: a 20-cm-thick layer is reduced to 4 or 5 cm thick after steaming. In the morning it was lifted out, cut into loaves, and divided among those who collected and prepared it.

Cooked lichen could be eaten immediately or dried and stored for future use. Dried lichen cakes would last three or more years if well preserved. They had to be soaked to make them soft before they could be eaten. Another method of cooking Black Tree Lichen, used by the Okanagan, was to roast it until dry and crumbly, then boil it until it was like molasses.

Cooked Black Tree Lichen is bland. To add flavour, interior groups often cooked it in layers interspersed with "barbecuing onions" (Nodding Onions) or they mixed it with Saskatoon Berries or their juice after cooking. The Okanagan sometimes cooked it with the rhizomes of False Solomon's Seal. Some people added sugar (brown, white or even Douglas-fir sugar). The Carrier people mixed it with flour and baked it like a fruit cake; before the introduction of flour they cooked it with grease.

Dried lichen could be eaten in a number of ways: it could be dipped in broth or soup and eaten like a cracker, marinated in Saskatoon Berry juice or boiled in a soup. The Okanagan made a tasty dish by cooking it with Bitter-root, dough and fresh salmon eggs. The Nlaka'pamux boiled it with dried "Indian Carrots", Saskatoon Berries, the bulbs of Yellow Avalanche Lily, Tiger Lily and other root vegetables, deer fat, dried deer meat, or salmon eggs. On long journeys, people ate dried lichen cakes as a sustainer. According to one source, Okanagan mothers fed their weaned babies a syrup made from Black Tree Lichen: "This was good for them." A.B. Chamberlain, in his "Report on the Kootenay people of south-eastern British Columbia" (1892) states that the Ktunaxa people mixed Black Tree Lichen with Wolf Lichen, which has a high concentration of vulpinic acid, but this is not substantiated by present Ktunaxa people. Many people have noted that Black Tree

Pine Mushroom

(Tricholoma Family)

Tricholoma magnivelare
(Peck) Redhead
(Tricholomataceae)

Other Names: American Matsutake, Wood Mushroom, Japanese Mushroom, Mountain Mushroom.

Botanical Description

Pine Mushroom grows 10 to 15 cm high, alone or in groups or clumps. The cap is white to pinkish buff when young, and becomes brownish with age; convex at first, it expands until it is nearly flat. The surface of the cap is dry to slightly sticky, and often has sand or conifer needles sticking to it. The margin of the cap is inrolled under a slightly persistent veil. The flesh is white and firm, with an agreeable, spicy odour and taste. The gills, spaced close together, run down the stem, or break free at maturity; they are whitish when young, become buff with age, and turn brown when bruised. The stem, 2 to 4 cm thick and 10 to 15 cm long, is the same colour as the cap and bears a single often upturned ring above the midpoint. The spores are white. *Tricholoma magnivelare* is also known as *Armillaria ponderosa*.

Pine Mushrooms prepared for eating.

Habitat: on ground in sandy soil under coniferous trees such as pines, Douglas-fir, Western Hemlock and Western Red-cedar. Pine Mushrooms are often hidden under a layer of needles and twigs, with only a mound to show where they are, or a small portion of cap exposed.

Distribution in British Columbia: common from September to December in conifer forests along coastal British Columbia and in parts of the interior; also in central and eastern Canada, and in Alberta and the Northwest Territories.

Aboriginal Use

The Nlaka'pamux and Stl'atl'imx peoples along the Fraser River have traditionally gathered Pine Mushrooms for a long time. In both Lower Nlaka'pamux and Lower Stl'atl'imx dialects, the general name for mushroom is synonymous with the name for this species. People locate the mushrooms from the mounds they produce in the tree litter, and carefully cut them at the base of the stem, so as not to disturb young emerging mushrooms nearby. Nlaka'pamux elder Annie York cautioned harvesters to carefully re-cover with soil those too young to pick and leave them to mature. People scrape clean the caps and stems of the harvested mushrooms and cut them into pieces. They cook the mushrooms and eat them fresh, or preserve them. Today, people sauté and freeze or jar them; formerly, they sliced them, strung them and hung them up to dry. Some people give Pine Mushrooms as gifts to elders and others who enjoy traditional foods. Now they are a valuable commodity, and some people – even those who did not pick them traditionally, such as the Ulkatcho and Tsilhqot'in – earn a good income by picking them and selling them to buyers for the Japanese market. Canadians and Americans of Japanese ancestry also harvest large quantities of these mushrooms and value them highly.

Cottonwood Mushroom

(Tricholoma Family)

Tricholoma populinum
J.E. Lange
(Tricholomataceae)

Other Name: Poplar Tricholoma.

Botanical Description
Cottonwood Mushroom is a medium-sized mushroom with a rounded to flattened, buff-coloured cap 7 to 12 cm across. It grows singly or in clusters. The colour of the cap varies from light brown at the edges to reddish brown towards the centre. The flesh is white or pale yellowish, staining reddish brown when bruised, and has a pleasant, distinctive odour.

The gills are white and notched near the stem. They are closely spaced, and like the flesh, stain pale reddish brown when old or bruised. The stem is up to 2 cm thick, slightly larger at the base, and 4 to 7 cm long. It is white but ages to reddish brown. The spores are white.

Habitat: grows singly or clustered in sandy soil under cottonwood trees in September and October. Cottonwood Mushrooms are often completely hidden by sand and leaves, and can be detected only by the mounds they produce when growing.

Distribution in British Columbia: widespread under cottonwood and other poplars in B.C. and across North America and Europe.

Aboriginal Use
The Cottonwood Mushroom was described and named by Interior Salish elders, and descriptions of it appeared in early ethnographic and ethnobotanical accounts, but it was not identified by its scientific classification until the early 1980s. In October 1982, Nlaka'pamux elder Hilda Austin took nutritionist Harriet Kuhnlein and me to collect Cottonwood Mushrooms. She showed us how to find, harvest, clean and cook them. Later, mycologist Keith Egger identified samples of these mushrooms and others collected with other Nlaka'pamux and

Stl'atl'imx elders. This mushroom and its use by Interior Salish peoples is described in detail in "The Cottonwood Mushroom" (Turner et al. 1985). Okanagan and Secwepemc people also ate these mushrooms, and some people still go out to harvest them every year around Thanksgiving time after the first heavy fall rain.

The best place to search for the Cottonwood Mushroom is on sandy ground under cottonwood trees, along rivers and lake shores. Hilda Austin took us to such a place. She carried a stick to push aside the leaves to reveal the mushrooms, which sometimes were in dense clusters. She checked the mushrooms for firmness, then whacked the cap sharply with the flat part of a knife to remove adhering sand. Later, in her kitchen, Hilda peeled the brownish skin off the cap, pulling it from the margin inwards, then scraped the stems to remove any sand. She separated the stems and caps and washed them in cold water, squeezing the soaked caps like a sponge to get rid of excess water. Then she fried them in hot lard until they were golden brown. They tasted delicious. While they were still hot, Hilda packaged some mushrooms up and we took them over to the local hospital to some of her elderly friends who were patients there. To them, freshly cooked Cottonwood Mushrooms were the best gift anyone could bring.

Interior Salish peoples traditionally sliced and dried Cottonwood Mushrooms for winter storage, then used them in soups and stews to add flavouring and texture. Today, people preserve them, as they do Pine Mushrooms, by freezing or jarring after lightly sautéing them. Nlaka'pamux sometimes washed new-born babies in the juice of Cottonwood Mushrooms. People said this bath would give the baby strength and independence, just as the mushroom, though soft, can push its way up through the sand, split open logs and dislodge rocks – its soft appearance is deceiving.

FERNS
(Pteridophyta)

Bracken Fern	*Pteridium aquilinum* (L.) Kuhn
(Fern Family)	(Polypodiaceae)

Botanical Description

The largest, most common fern in the province, Bracken Fern often grows over 150 cm tall. The rhizomes are perennial, often 20 cm deep, running horizontally for long distances, frequently branching. They are

round in cross-section, about as thick as a man's middle finger, black outside, white and glutinous inside, with tough longitudinal fibres in the centre. Fronds grow individually along the rhizome, having tall, smooth, light-green stems and coarsely branching pinnae. The fronds and lower pinnae are broadly triangular in shape. Pinnules are numerous and deeply toothed; and sori, when present, are marginal and mostly continuous.

Habitat: usually in open forests and clearings at lower and middle elevations.

Distribution in British Columbia: generally throughout the province, except at high elevations.

Aboriginal Use

Interior First Peoples did not use ferns as food nearly as much as coastal peoples did. Bracken rhizomes, an almost universal food on the coast, were eaten by only a few interior groups, mostly those in areas near the coast, notably the Lower Stl'atl'imx at Pemberton and the Lower Nlaka'pamux of the Fraser Canyon. The Carrier also ate the rhizomes, but not the Tsilhqot'in, according to Father Morice in his writings on the Déné; apparently, the Sekani ate them as well.

Bracken Fern rhizomes.

The Pemberton Stl'atl'imx dug Bracken rhizomes in early spring, when the tops were just beginning to sprout. They roasted them in hot coals, until the outer "bark" had burned away, then peeled off the inner skin and pulverized the white inner part, removing the tough central fibres. They ate it "just like candy" or formed it into loaves. They believed that the central fibrous "veins" would cause paralysis if eaten. Bracken rhizomes were a major food of early spring in the Pemberton area.

The Nlaka'pamux ate bracken rhizomes raw, or they peeled, roasted and pounded them into flour. Some people also ate the young fiddle-heads (shoots) raw, a use they may have learned from local Japanese settlers, who also ate them. They soaked the fiddleheads in salt water overnight to remove the bitterness. (See the Warning below.)

The Carrier people steam-cooked the rhizomes in underground pits for 10 to 12 hours and ate them with meat or fish. According to available information, the rhizomes were not eaten by other interior groups, even in areas such as Secwepemc and Ktunaxa territory, where bracken is abundant.

Other fern species used peripherally by interior First Peoples are listed in Appendix 1.

Warning
Bracken leaves and hay contaminated with Bracken are known to be poisonous to livestock when eaten in large quantities. The toxic ingredient is an enzyme, thiaminase, which destroys the animal's thiamine reserves. Judging from the widespread use of Bracken rhizomes and fiddleheads as food, this enzyme is not present in significant quantities in these parts of the plant. But there is more recent evidence that eating Bracken fronds can cause cancer. For more information on the toxic qualities of Bracken, read the entry in *Common Poisonous Plants and Mushrooms of North America* (Turner and Szczawinski 1991).

CONIFERS
(Pinitae)

Rocky Mountain Juniper   *Juniperus scopulorum* Sarg.
Common Juniper   *J. communis* L.
(Cypress Family)   (Cupressaceae)

Botanical Description
Rocky Mountain Juniper usually grows as a dense tree up to 10 metres tall, although it can also be found as a sprawling shrub less than a metre tall. It has stringy, reddish-brown bark and scale-like leaves. Common Juniper usually grows as a prostrate, trailing shrub, with shredding reddish-brown bark and stiff needle-like leaves 7 to 12 mm long. Both species are dioecious – producing male and female cones on separate plants. The female cones, the size of small peas, are blue to bluish-black and berry-like, though hard and pungent smelling. They are usually covered with a whitish waxy coating, giving them a grey hue. They take two seasons to mature.

Rocky Mountain Juniper.

Common Juniper.

Habitat: Rocky Mountain Juniper grows on coastal islands, dry plains and lower mountains, and in valleys; Common Juniper is found in open woods and valleys and on dry hills and open rocky slopes from near sea-level to subalpine or alpine areas.

Distribution in British Columbia: Rocky Mountain Juniper grows in dry sites from coastal Vancouver Island and the Gulf Islands eastward to the Rocky Mountains and north to the Peace and Stikine rivers; Common Juniper grows in mountains throughout the province, and also on the dry plains of the Interior Plateau.

Aboriginal Use

Most aboriginal peoples in the province used junipers as fumigants, deodorizers and cleansers, especially in connection with sickness. The pungent smell of the boughs, when burned or brewed on a stove, was said to purify a house in which there had been illness or death, protecting the inhabitants from infection and harmful spirits.

The use of juniper as food was rather limited. The "berries" were seldom eaten, being strong-tasting and pitchy, but the Stl'atl'imx considered Rocky Mountain Juniper berries edible if not too many were eaten at once. They believed that chewing a few berries or a small piece of the bitter bark would keep one from getting hungry all day. A number of groups, including Nlaka'pamux, Stl'atl'imx, Carrier and Ktunaxa, boiled the branches and berries of both species to make tea, but they usually drank it only as a medicine (for colds, tuberculosis, or heart trouble) and seldom just as a beverage.

Juniper fruit is well known in North America and Europe as a flavouring for gin and beer and as a culinary spice.

Warning

Junipers are known to have diuretic properties. Drink only moderate amounts of juniper tea; pregnant women should not drink it at all, as it may cause uterine contractions.

Western Larch
(Pine Family)

Larix occidentalis Nutt.
(Pinaceae)

Other Names: Tamarack, Western Tamarack.

Botanical Description
Western Larch is a large, handsome tree that grows up to 70 metres tall, with thick, flaky cinnamon-coloured bark; a mature tree has few branches on its lower trunk. The pale green, needle-like leaves, 4 to 5 cm long, grow in clusters of 15 to 30. Unlike most conifer needles, the leaves of Western Larch are deciduous, turning golden yellow and dropping in autumn. The yellowish male cones are about 1 cm long, and the female cones are 3 to 4 cm long, at first purplish red, later reddish brown.

Habitat: mountain valleys and lower slopes, often in somewhat swampy areas, usually in mixed stands.

Distribution in British Columbia: on north slopes and in higher valleys of the Kootenay, Arrow and Okanagan drainage systems, from the United States border north as far as Shuswap Lake.

Aboriginal Use
Western Larch exudes a sweet-tasting gum that hardens on exposure to the air. The Nlaka'pamux, Okanagan, Ktunaxa and others broke off and chewed the gum for pleasure at any time of the year. It is said to taste just like candy. The Ktunaxa and the Flathead Salish of Montana

Western Larch
with Black Tree
Lichen hanging
from its branches.

ate the cambium (the slimy layer between the bark and wood) in spring. These two groups also obtained a kind of syrup from natural or human-made reservoirs in certain trees. A good syrup-producing tree might yield as much as a gallon of liquid once or twice a year. The Flathead evaporated the syrup until it had the consistency of molasses, but the Ktunaxa, at least within living memory, mixed it with sugar and used it as people might use syrup or honey today. The Flathead also harvested sap from hollowed-out cavities in Water Birch trees and drank it as a sweet beverage.

Whitebark Pine
(Pine Family)

Pinus albicaulis Engelm.
(Pinaceae)

Botanical Description

Whitebark Pine is a gnarled dwarf tree or sprawling shrub seldom over 9 metres high and 50 cm in trunk diameter, with thin, light-grey, scaly bark. The leaves are yellow-green, 4 to 8 cm long, in clusters of five. The male cones are small and red. The oval-shaped female cones are 5 to 8 cm long, deep red, purplish, or grey, and tend to remain closed, seldom falling from the tree intact. The seeds are large, 8 to 12 mm long, brown and wingless.

Habitat: subalpine to the timber-line, on ridge-tops and exposed rocky slopes; rarely found below 1,200 metres.

Distribution in British Columbia: near the tree-line in mountains throughout the southern interior (south of 54°N latitude).

Aboriginal Use

The interior First Peoples of British Columbia ate Whitebark Pine seeds or "nuts" in much the same way as the First Peoples of the southwestern United States ate piñon pine nuts (from low-growing pines such as

shaken), the cambium is thick and juicy. After the bark is removed, the cambium can be scraped from the wood in long, fleshy ribbons, about 3 cm wide and 60 cm long. Most groups preferred to collect it at this time, using scrapers made of Caribou antler, deer ulna, or the shoulder blade of a Black Bear. Collectors held a basket at the base of the tree, and scraped off the cambium from bottom to top so none of the juice would be lost. Certain trees, notably those of the montane regions in damper sites, yielded more cambium than others.

The Okanagan sometimes harvested the cambium at a slightly later stage, when it had become separated from the wood and stuck to the inside of the bark. They removed the bark, with the cambium attached, laid it on the ground, and scraped off the cambium with a deer-rib scraper.

Most groups ate pine cambium fresh, as it was gathered, but some, notably the Secwepemc, sometimes dried it for later use. The Ktunaxa thought cambium to be especially good for people with consumption, and the Carrier believed it to be a good medicine for colds. It is seldom eaten today; when it is, it is harvested with a steel knife, or with a flat metal scraper, often cut from a tin can. Bears are said to relish pine cambium. Sometimes you can see trees where they have been scratching for it. It makes their fur matted and sticky.

Interior First Peoples in some localities harvested the cambium of several other trees, including Ponderosa Pine, White Pine, Whitebark Pine, Subalpine Fir, Trembling Aspen, Black Cottonwood and Paper Birch.

Note
Tree cambium can be a valuable source of nourishment in an emergency, but to collect it you must remove the bark, which is harmful to the tree – fatal if the tree is completely girdled. Cambium should be harvested only with the greatest discrimination.

Ponderosa Pine
(Pine Family)

Pinus ponderosa Dougl. ex Laws.
(Pinaceae)

Other Names: Yellow Pine, Red Pine, Bull Pine.

Botanical Description

Ponderosa Pine is a large forest tree, commonly 30 metres or more tall, with thick reddish furrowed bark that flakes off in irregular scales. Its yellowish-green needles, usually growing in clusters of three, are longer than those of any other conifer in British Columbia, frequently more than 20 cm long. They are usually clustered toward the branch ends, giving the tree a feathery appearance. The male pollen cones are yellow to purplish and strongly clustered, and the female seed cones are broadly oval-shaped, reddish-purple when young, and brown when they mature after two years. The seeds are 6 to 7 mm long, with prominent wings to aid in dispersal.

Habitat: dry, warm valleys and slopes up to 900 metres; intolerant of shade and extreme cold.

Distribution in British Columbia: forming open parklike forests in the dry southern interior east of the Cascade Mountains, from the Fraser and Thompson river canyons to the Okanagan and Similkameen valleys, as far north as Clinton in the Cariboo; recurring in the dry sections of the Kootenay and Columbia river valleys.

Aboriginal Use

The Nlaka'pamux, Okanagan, southern Secwepemc and Ktunaxa peoples collected and ate Ponderosa Pine cambium in the same manner as Lodgepole Pine cambium. The Flathead Salish of Montana used it more than that of Lodgepole Pine. The best cambium came from young Ponderosa Pines, before they began to bear cones. It could also be taken from the twigs and branches of older trees. Ponderosa Pine cambium was usually ready to harvest two or three weeks before

Ponderosa and Whitebark pine seeds.

Lodgepole Pine cambium, and could be eaten fresh or roasted.

The above groups and the Stl'atl'imx also ate Ponderosa Pine seeds, just as they ate White-bark Pine seeds. They gathered them in the fall, either when they were released from cones still on the trees and came floating to the ground on their wings "like but-terflies", or from cones cut down prematurely by squirrels. People took squirrel-cut cones home and dried them until the scales opened, then shook the seeds out. They cracked open the seeds and ate them raw. "Once you start eating them you can't quit," remarked one Secwepemc woman, citing a common problem of nut-eaters everywhere. Although Ponderosa Pine seeds were popular, especially with children, they were seldom regarded as anything more than a snack; collecting them was too painstaking and time-consuming in relation to their food value for them to become a regular part of the diet.

The Okanagan and others chewed the reddish pitch like gum.

Douglas-fir (Pine Family) — *Pseudotsuga menziesii* (Mirbel) Franco (Pinaceae)

Other Names: Oregon Pine; simply "fir" to many aboriginal people.

Botanical Description

A giant forest tree, Douglas-fir grows up to 70 metres high on the coast, but seldom more than 40 metres in the interior. The bark of young trees is smooth and grey-brown, often with resin-blisters, but on old trees it becomes thick and furrowed, grey outside, and mottled red-brown and whitish inside. The needles are flat, pointed, but not prickly, 2 to 3 cm long, uniformly spaced along the twig and spreading from the sides and top. The pollen cones are small and reddish-brown. The seed cones, which hang from the branches, are green before maturity, then reddish-brown to grey; they fall soon after maturing. Prominent, three-pointed bracts extend well beyond the cone scales. Cones of coastal trees are mostly 6 to 10 cm long, whereas those of interior trees vary from 4 to 7 cm. The seeds are 5 to 6 mm long, with prominent wings. Coastal and interior populations form two well-defined geographic races, designated as *P. menziesii* var. *menziesii* and *P. menziesii* var. *glauca* respectively.

Habitat: moist to very dry areas, from sea level to 1 500 metres in the southern interior, and as high as 1 800 metres in the Rocky Mountains.

Distribution in British Columbia: widespread throughout the southern half of the province, extending as far north as Stuart and McLeod lakes and up the Parsnip River in the interior. Does not occur on Haida Gwaii or most of the central and northern coast.

Aboriginal Use

The Secwepemc occasionally ate the small, pitchy seeds of Douglas-fir, especially if they found them in the caches of squirrels or mice. The Nlaka'pamux made a tea with tonic properties from the young twigs and needles. And the Ktunaxa pulled off pieces of the dried sap and chewed it like gum – this was especially good for treating colds.

But the most interesting type of food obtained from Douglas-fir was a white crystalline substance that forms on the leaves and branches of some trees in special circumstances. Known as "Douglas-fir sugar" or "wild sugar", this rare material had a reputation far exceeding its abundance. The Nlaka'pamux, Stl'atl'imx and Secwepemc, as well as some groups in eastern Washington, used this sugar whenever they could find it. Some old-timers of the present day remember seeing it or hearing of it, but it is said to have become even less common than it used to be.

According to John Davidson (1919), who worked with ethnographer James Teit on this sugar, it occurs in the interior dry-belt zone on trees that are well exposed to the sun and have good soil moisture during the hottest days of summer. It is formed when cell fluid is exuded from the tips of the needles as a result of high photosynthetic activity, high root pressure and a low rate of transpiration in the leaves. The sugar appears as white globules "like ice over the branches". It tastes sweet and dissolves in the mouth. Interestingly, it contains, along with sucrose and

Douglas-fir sugar, collected by James Teit (from Davidson 1919).

reducing sugars, a rare trisaccharide sugar known as melezitose, which amounts to more than 50 per cent of its constituents.

As might be expected, Douglas-fir sugar, being so sporadic in its occurrence, was not a staple food of the aboriginal peoples who used it; rather, it was eaten as a confection when encountered, or, if there was a sufficient quantity, it was collected in a container to take home to use over the winter. It was sometimes used as a sweetener mixed with other foods such as Black Tree Lichen and Balsamroot seeds.

FLOWERING PLANTS
(Angiospermae)
MONOCOTYLEDONS

Skunk Cabbage

(Arum Family)

Lysichitum americanum
Hultén & St. John
(Araceae)

Other Names: Yellow Arum, Swamp Lantern.

Botanical Description
Skunk Cabbage is a perennial herb with thick, fleshy rootstocks and large, clustered, oval leaves, mostly 40 to 100 cm long, bright green and waxy. Flowers appear in early spring, consisting of a bright yellow sheath, up to 20 cm long, surrounding a club-like, yellowish-green flower stalk. At maturity the stalk breaks apart to reveal brown oval seeds embedded in a white pulpy tissue. The skunk-like odour of this plant resembles that of the closely related *Symplocarpus foetidus* of eastern North America.

Habitat: swampy ground, especially black mucky soil, beneath alder and cedar; rarely flowers in dense shade.

Distribution in British Columbia: common in coastal forests and swampy areas from Vancouver Island to Alaska and east to the Columbia River, but not in arid or semi-arid areas; extends as far north as 54°N latitude in the eastern part of the province.

Aboriginal Use

The Lower Stl'atl'imx of the Pemberton area, who were culturally and geographically transitional between the coast and interior, used to eat the long white rhizomes of Skunk Cabbage. Other interior peoples, such as the Secwepemc, also ate the rhizomes, and some used the leaves, as the coastal peoples did, for lining steaming pits and for laying food on. At Pemberton, Skunk Cabbage rhizomes were the first vegetable food to be gathered in the early spring. The Lower Stl'atl'imx dug the rhizomes, up to 25 cm long and 3 cm thick, with sharp sticks, then washed and boiled or steamed them in underground pits. The rhizomes were named after their taste, "hot, like pepper". The Pemberton Stl'atl'imx have not eaten the rhizomes for several generations.

Warning

Skunk Cabbage, like many other members of the arum family, contains long sharp crystals of calcium oxalate. If you put any part of a Skunk Cabbage into your mouth, the crystals can become embedded in your mucus membranes and provoke intense irritation and burning. Prolonged cooking and storage reduces the effects of these crystals, but do not eat the roots without cooking them first and never eat the mature leaves, raw or cooked.

Nodding Onion	*Allium cernuum* **Roth**
Hooker's Onion	*A. acuminatum* **Hook.**
Other Wild Onions	*Allium* **spp.**
(Lily Family)	**(Liliaceae)**

Botanical Description

All these wild onions are herbaceous perennials with a characteristic onion odour, round or elongated bulbs, grass-like leaves and small flowers clustered in an umbrella-like head. Nodding Onion has tapering pink-coated clustered bulbs; the leaves remain green during flowering; the flower stems are 10 to 50 cm long, with distinctly nodding flower heads. Hooker's Onion has small spherical bulbs with a brownish net-like outer skin; its short leaves wither before the flowers appear; its flower stems are 10 to 30 cm long. The flowers of both species are

Hooker's Onion (above)
and Nodding Onion (right).

pinkish to rose-purple, but other wild onions have white flowers. True onions can be distinguished from other bulb-bearing plants, such as Fool's Onion, Mariposa Lily and "Poison Onion" (Death Camas), by their unmistakable onion smell.

Habitat: rocky crevices and sandy soil in open woods and exposed areas.

Distribution in British Columbia: generally throughout the province, except on Haida Gwaii. Nodding Onion is the most common species, ranging from the Pacific coast to the dry interior, the Kootenays and the Cariboo, at least as far as 56°N latitude. Hooker's Onion is restricted to the dry slopes of the southern coastal forests west of the Cascade Range.

Aboriginal Use
The bulbs of Nodding Onion were a popular food in the interior, even more than they were on the coast. All the interior Salish groups ate them, as did the Ktunaxa, Carrier, Wet'suwet'en, Sekani and Dene-thah, and probably other Athapaskan groups as well. The Lower Nlaka'pamux and Lower Stl'atl'imx situated within the range of Hooker's Onion ate the bulbs of this species also. Interior First Peoples also

Nodding Onion bulbs.

used other species, such as Geyer's Onion, which grows at Botanie Valley, and Wild Chives, which grows in the Kootenays and northern British Columbia.

Nodding Onion bulbs, clustered and shallow-growing, were harvested in large quantities during the spring, from May to July, before the flowers appeared. They could be eaten raw, leaves and all, but usually they were bundled or woven together by their leaves and steam-cooked in underground pits overnight. The Nlaka'pamux sometimes interspersed them with layers of leafy branches from Shrubby Penstemon and Red Alder, and sometimes covered them with scrapings of alder bark to give them a reddish colour. The Stl'atl'imx cleaned them by rubbing them with Shrubby Penstemon, then cooked them interspersed with the branches of Saskatoon Berry or other shrubs, and rye-grass or bunchgrass. The Okanagan used branches and "Timbergrass" (apparently Pinegrass) in their steaming pits. The Secwepemc also cooked Nodding Onions in pits or simply roasted them in an open fire.

Nodding Onions are strong smelling and strong tasting (the Carrier name means "stink grass"), a characteristic which made them ideal for flavouring other food. They were frequently pit-cooked, interspersed with layers of Black Tree Lichen, and the Okanagan mixed them with Blue Camas bulbs and other roots for cooking. They were also used to flavour meat and salmon. But many aboriginal people testify that, once properly cooked, the onions lose their strong smell and flavour, becoming sweet and nearly black in colour. Stl'atl'imx elder Sam Mitchell declared that he had never tasted anything better than freshly cooked "barbecuing onions". Once cooked, the onions can be eaten immediately, or dried by braiding or stringing them together, pressing them into thin cakes or simply laying them out on mats. The dried bulbs are reconstituted by sprinkling water on them, or by soaking or boiling them.

The Lower Nlaka'pamux and Lower Stl'atl'imx gathered Hooker's Onions in late fall or early spring and prepared them in much the same manner as Nodding Onions.

Warning

Wild onion bulbs may be confused with those of Death Camas (*Zigadenus venenosus*), discussed in Appendix 4. The safest distinction is the characteristic onion odour of true wild onion plants.

Fool's Onion

(Lily Family)

Brodiaea hyacinthina (Lindl.) Baker and *B. douglasii* Wats.
(Liliaceae)

Other Names: Cluster Lily, Brodiaea.

Botanical Description

Fool's Onions are herbaceous perennials with globular straw-coloured corms, flattened grass-like leaves, slender erect stems and terminal flowers in umbrella-like clusters. *Brodiaea hyacinthina* has white flowers, and *B. douglasii* has blue. *B. hyacinthina* is also known as *Triteleia hyacinthina* and *B. douglasii* is also known as *T. grandiflora*.

Habitat: *B. hyacinthina* grows in meadows and grassy open flats that are often rocky, from valleys to middle elevations; *B. douglasii* is found in grasslands and sagebrush deserts, as well as Ponderosa Pine woodlands.

Distribution in British Columbia: *B. hyacinthina* is found in southern British Columbia west of the Cascade Mountains and eastward along the Fraser River canyon; *B. douglasii* is common in the southern interior.

Aboriginal Use

The Nlaka'pamux and Stl'atl'imx, especially those in the Fraser River canyon and around Pemberton, ate the corms of *B. hyacinthina*. They harvested them in April, at the same time as Yellowbell bulbs – the first roots to be dug in spring. In the previous year, the gatherers had marked the places where the plants grew, so they could find this year's crop of corms even before the leaves appeared. They ate Fool's Onion corms raw or boiled and dried. The Nlaka'pamux once ate the corms of *B. douglasii*, but were not using them as of about 1920.

Warning
Fool's Onion corms can be confused with the bulbs of Death Camas (*Zigadenus venenosus*), discussed in Appendix 4. Never eat any wild bulbs or corms without being absolutely sure what they are.

Mariposa Lily   *Calochortus macrocarpus* Dougl.
(Lily Family)   (Liliaceae)

Other Names: Desert Lily, Lavender Lily, Sego Lily, Sagebrush Mariposa, "Wild Gladiola", "Sweet Onion", "Wild Potato".

Botanical Description
Mariposa Lily is a herbaceous perennial with a tapering deep-seated bulb, blue-green grass-like leaves that wither before the plant flowers and an erect, usually unbranched stem. It has striking lavender-to-pink three-petalled flowers up to 5 cm across, borne singly or in twos or threes at the top. Each petal is marked with a central longitudinal green stripe and usually a transverse band of dark purple toward the base. The sepals, also three per flower, are lance-shaped and longer than the petals. The bases of the petals are densely covered with whitish fuzz. The plants usually bloom in June. The seed capsules are erect, narrow, tapered and scarcely winged.

Habitat: dry hillsides and plains, usually in light sandy soil.

Distribution in British Columbia: east of the Coast and Cascade mountains, south of Williams Lake, in the Interior Plateau and the

Columbia and Kootenay river valleys. Another species with white flowers, known as the Three-spot Tulip, is found in the Rocky Mountain Trench from Windermere south.

Aboriginal Use

All the interior Salish groups, the Ktunaxa and the Tsilhqot'in ate the small elongated bulbs of Mariposa Lily, which they often called "Sweet Onions" or "Wild Potatoes"; the Ktunaxa also ate the bulbs of the Three-spot Tulip. People harvested Mariposa Lily bulbs in the spring, from April to June, usually before the plants flowered. The bulbs are crisp and sweet, so people usually ate them raw, but if they collected enough, threaded and dried them, with or without steaming them first. The Okanagan sometimes cooked them with other foods as a flavouring. Mariposa Lily bulbs are still eaten today in some areas, although their numbers are rapidly diminishing, mainly due to over-grazing by cattle and sheep. Now, people steam them in saucepans on top of the stove and serve them hot as a vegetable. Some people preserve them by canning.

The Nlaka'pamux, and perhaps some other groups, once ate the flower buds as well. They ate them raw, appreciating the sweet nectar at the base of the petals.

Note

Mariposa Lily is becoming rare in some areas, as a result of habitat destruction and overgrazing by livestock. In the past, people ate the bulbs in large quantities; but today, discretion is advised. Digging up a bulb destroys the whole plant.

Blue Camas
(Lily Family)

Camassia quamash (Pursh) Greene
(Liliaceae)

Other Names: Sweet Camas, Edible Camas, "Black Camas".

Botanical Description
Blue Camas is a herbaceous perennial with glutinous bulbs about the size of daffodil bulbs, covered with a membranous brown skin. The leaves are grass-like, 10-15 mm broad and up to 50 cm long. The flower stems are erect, 20 to 70 cm tall, bearing a loose terminal cluster of showy deep blue to light blue or white blossoms in late spring (May to June).

Habitat: grassy meadows and bluffs, often in moist or swampy fields in the interior.

Distribution in British Columbia: common on southeastern Vancouver Island and the Gulf Islands, recurring in the Columbia River valley south of Castlegar and in southern Alberta; widespread in parts of eastern Washington and Idaho. A second, more robust species, *Camassia leichtlinii*, is found in Canada only in southwestern British Columbia, west of the Cascade Mountains.

Aboriginal Use
Camas bulbs were a staple food for the Coast Salish of southern Vancouver Island and the Gulf Islands, as discussed in *Food Plants of Coastal First Peoples*. Although the natural range of camas in the interior is extremely limited, its distribution was significantly increased through trade with aboriginal groups of Washington, Idaho and Montana, where it was a staple food. Hence, it was known not only to the Ktunaxa but also, at least in dried form, to the Okanagan, Nlaka'pamux and southern Secwepemc of British Columbia.

The Southern Okanagan of Washington were major suppliers of camas to the British Columbia Salish groups. They recognize several types of camas, of which *Camassia* or "Black Camas" was only one. The others, known as "White Camas", "Little White Camas", or simply

"Camas", were species of *Lomatium* in the celery family (Apiaceae). *Camassia* bulbs are the sweetest kind of camas, tasting, according to some sources, like sweet chestnuts. In former times, a large portion of the Southern Okanagans' supply of *Camassia* was obtained by trade from Idaho and Montana. (See the photograph of camas bulbs from Washington, with Bitter-roots and Biscuitroots, on page 82.)

In the areas where Blue Camas grows, people dug the bulbs after the plants had flowered, from May to early August, depending upon the elevation. They cleaned them, then steamed them in pits for up to three days, until the bulbs were hard and blackish, or they dried the bulbs on mats, without cooking them. Sometimes they ate cooked Blue Camas bulbs with other foods, such as Black Tree Lichen, Nodding Onions, Bitter-root, deer meat or salmon. The Flathead ground cooked camas bulbs with a stone pestle or, more recently, a meat grinder, and made them into small cakes to be eaten with flour, cream and sugar; they also boiled camas down to make a gravy with flour or into a sweet, hot beverage.

Warning
Care must be taken never to confuse the bulbs of Blue Camas with those of the closely related Death Camas (*Zigadenus venenosus*). Death Camas commonly grows together with Blue Camas, and the leaves are difficult to distinguish. Also, the bulbs are similar in size and shape. But Death Camas has cream-coloured flowers that are smaller and in a tighter cluster than those of the two Blue Camas species. Anyone wishing to sample Blue Camas bulbs should dig them up at flowering time to avoid any possibility of misidentification. Death Camas is discussed in Appendix 4.

Yellow Avalanche Lily

(Lily Family)

Erythronium grandiflorum Pursh
(Liliaceae)

Other Names: Glacier Lily, Yellow Dog-tooth Violet, Snow Lily, Dog-tooth Lily, "Indian Sweet Potato", "Indian Potato".

Botanical Description
Yellow Avalanche Lily is a herbaceous perennial with an elongated, deeply buried corm-like bulb. The plant usually bears two basal, lance-shaped to elliptical leaves, acutely pointed and tapered at the base. The flower stem is erect, usually about 15 cm high, bearing one, two, or sometimes more nodding golden-yellow flowers. The flowers are up to 5 cm across with prominent stamens and pistil; at maturity, the petals strongly recurve. Blooming season is from April to August, depending on the elevation. The seed capsule is club-shaped, about 3 cm long and contains many brown seeds.

Habitat: moist upland meadows, avalanche chutes and open woods.

Distribution in British Columbia: in mountains and high valleys from Vancouver Island to the Rocky Mountains, south of 53°N latitude; abundant at relatively low elevations in some localities, such as the areas around Chase and Shuswap Lake.

Aboriginal Use
The slender starchy bulbs of Yellow Avalanche Lily rank with Bitterroot, wild onions and Spring Beauty in importance as a food source for the First Peoples of the southern interior. They were eaten in large quantities by the Nlaka'pamux, Stl'atl'imx, Okanagan, Secwepemc and Carrier. The Ktunaxa may also have used them, but this remains to be confirmed.

In the valley bottoms at lower elevations, people dug up Yellow Avalanche Lily bulbs in April and May, when the leaves and flower buds first appeared; on higher ridges and north-facing slopes the bulbs were not ready until later in the summer. One of the prime localities for gathering Yellow Avalanche Lily bulbs was Botanie Valley, north of Lytton. This area belonged to the Nlaka'pamux people of Lytton, and still does*. They hosted the many families from different parts of the country who journeyed there each year to

Yellow Avalanche Lily bulbs, ready for cooking.

partake in the harvest of these and other wild vegetables. In Secwepemc country, a good location for digging the bulbs is in the vicinity of Adams Lake, northwest of Shuswap Lake. Here a family might gather a hundred kilograms or more, considered a good winter's supply.

When people wanted to eat Yellow Avalanche Lily bulbs immediately, they steamed them, roasted them in hot ashes, or boiled them for a short time. To preserve the bulbs for winter, they let them soften for a few days, then peeled and threaded them on a string of twisted Western Red-cedar or Rocky Mountain Maple bark and hung them up to dry, until they were hard and tan coloured. Circular strings of avalanche lily bulbs, usually of measured length from hand to elbow, were an important trading item. The bulbs could also be dried unstrung and stored in sacks. To prepare the dried bulbs for eating, people soaked them until they had regained most of their moisture, then boiled or steamed them in underground pits until they were soft and chocolate-brown. They are said to taste sweet.

Yellow Avalanche Lily bulbs are little used today, but some people still dig them up and enjoy them on special occasions. They grow deep in the ground and are extremely difficult to harvest, especially in rocky soils. One modern method of cooking them is by deep-frying.

Warning
According to Kingsbury (1964), the corms of a related species, the White Fawn Lily or Easter Lily (*Erythronium oregonum*), were implicated in poisoning of poultry in Vancouver.

---

* The main part of Botanie Valley is aboriginal reserve land and cannot be entered without the permission of the Lytton Band.

Chocolate Lily
(Lily Family)

Fritillaria lanceolata Pursh
(Liliaceae)

Other Names: Rice Root, "Indian Rice".

Botanical Description
Chocolate Lily is a herbaceous perennial with a white bell-shaped bulb covered with rice-like bulblets. The stems are single, slender and 20 to 50 cm tall, with usually two whorls of narrow, tapering leaves. The flowers are borne singly or in loose clusters of two to five; they are nodding, bell-shaped, chocolate-brown to dark purple, and mottled with greenish-yellow specks. The flowers have a distinctly bad odour and are pollinated by carrion insects. The seed capsules are upright, angled and winged vertically. Chocolate Lily blooms from April to June. A closely related species, *Fritillaria camschatcensis,* found mostly along the coast, is also called Rice Root; it is taller and more robust, with a terminal cluster of unmottled dark, purple-brown flowers.

Habitat: meadows and grassy bluffs from sea level to high mountain valleys, such as Botanie. *F. camschatcensis* is found in damp clearings and salt marshes.

Distribution in British Columbia: in the southwest from the Okanagan Valley to the lower Fraser River valley and on Vancouver Island and the Gulf Islands. *F. camschatcensis* is common along the entire coast, but is also found inland along the Skeena and Bulkley river valleys.

Aboriginal Use
All interior Salish groups, except possibly the Okanagan and northern Secwepemc, ate Chocolate Lily bulbs. The Lower Stl'atl'imx of the

Pemberton area dug them up in late fall or early spring when the tops were just sprouting, whereas the Secwepemc and Nlaka'pamux harvested them from May to August, after the plants had flowered. People boiled them in soups or steamed them; the cooked bulbs are mild and soft, sometimes with a slightly bitter taste. Chocolate Lily bulbs were not usually dried for storage, although

Chocolate Lily bulb covered with rice-like bulblets.

they could be kept fresh for a short time in underground pits or root cellars. The Coast Salish of Vancouver Island and the Lower Mainland also ate the bulbs. The Secwepemc also apparently ate the stem portion.

The Nisga'a and Gitxsan, and probably the Wet'suwet'en, Carrier and Tsilhqot'in as well, ate the bulbs of the larger Rice Root (*F. camschatcensis*) as did the central and northern coastal peoples. The Nisga'a removed the rice-like bulblets, washed them, and boiled them without salt. They ate them with hemlock cambium cakes, Eulachon grease, and recently, sugar. Some people still use them.

Yellowbell   *Fritillaria pudica* (Pursh) Spreng.
(Lily Family)   (Liliaceae)

Other Name: Yellow Snowdrop.

Botanical Description
Yellowbell is a slender herbaceous perennial, 9 to 25 cm tall. The bulbs can be 3 cm long, but are usually smaller, and have two or more large, fleshy scales. The leaves are lance-shaped and bluish-green; they grow in clusters of two to eight around the mid-section of the stem. The flowers are terminal, nodding, bell-shaped and usually single; early blooming, from April to May, they are yellow, turning brick red with age. The fruit is a distinctive, club-shaped capsule, green and white striped when young, and up to 3 cm long.

Habitat: grasslands and sagebrush desert and open Ponderosa Pine or mixed coniferous forest.

Distribution in British Columbia: limited to the dry valleys of the southern interior, from Sicamous southward.

Aboriginal Use

The Nlaka'pamux, Okanagan and Secwepemc ate Yellowbell bulbs when available, but apparently the Ktunaxa and Stl'atl'imx did not. Some Stl'atl'imx people believed them to be poisonous. The Nlaka'pa-

mux dug up the bulbs in the early spring, at the same time as the corms of Fool's Onion. The Okanagan and Secwepemc harvested them in late spring or summer, often when they gathered Spring Beauty corms ("Indian Potatoes"). Yellowbell bulbs could be eaten raw, boiled or steamed for a short time. The Secwepemc sometimes stored them in underground pits with "Indian Potatoes", whereas the Southern Okanagan of Washington dried them on mats for up to two weeks, after which they would keep through the winter. The Nlaka'pamux and Northern Okanagan used them only sporadically and did not usually bother storing them.

Tiger Lily
(Lily Family)

Lilium columbianum Hanson
(Liliaceae)

Other Names: Columbia Lily, Panther Lily.

Botanical Description
Tiger Lily is a tall perennial with a white ovoid bulb, up to 5 cm in diameter, composed of thick, fleshy scales, like garlic cloves. The stem is slender, up to a metre long, with many whorls of narrow, lance-shaped leaves. The flowers are terminal, single to several, with bright orange recurved petals, dark-spotted near the centre. The seed capsules are oblong and tapered near the base. *Lilium columbianum* is also known as *L. parviflorum*. Another species, more restricted in range, is the Wood Lily (*L. philadelphicum*); it has large orange upright flowers, growing singly or in clusters of up to five.

Habitat: damp open woods and meadows, from sea level to subalpine elevations. Wood Lily is found in open woods and grassy places.

Distribution in British Columbia: throughout the province, south of latitude 54°N. Wood Lily is confined to the Columbia River valley, along the Kicking Horse River and in the Peace River District.

Tiger Lily flowers and bulbs.

Aboriginal Use

Interior First Peoples ate the large bulbs of Tiger Lily wherever they could find them, just as coastal peoples did. Tiger Lily bulbs are strong-tasting, peppery and bitter, but were very popular in the old days – apparently they are an acquired taste. Often they were accorded the status of a flavouring or condiment, like pepper or garlic, to enhance the taste of other foods. In a number of interior Salish languages, the name is derived from the word for "bitter".

The Carrier and Tsilhqot'in, who called this plant "beaver-stick", harvested the bulbs in early spring, as soon as the leaves had sprouted, just after the disappearance of the snow. The Nlaka'pamux and Stl'atl'imx also dug up the bulbs in spring, whereas the Secwepemc, Okanagan and Ktunaxa usually dug them up in late summer and fall, as late as November. According to James Teit, the largest bulbs to be obtained were in Secwepemc Territory, in the vicinity of Horsefly Lake, south of Quesnel Lake in the Cariboo District. Here, they might exceed a width of 7 cm. Tiger Lily bulbs are also abundant at Botanie Valley and around McGillivray Lake.

Because of their bitter quality, Tiger Lily bulbs were not usually eaten raw, but boiled, sometimes in two changes of water, or steamed for several hours. If people could gather enough, they would dry them in the sun after cooking, either whole or mashed in thin cakes, then store them for winter. People often ate boiled Tiger Lily bulbs with other foods, such as deer meat, fish, fermented salmon roe or Saskatoon Berries.

The late Nlaka'pamux elder Annie York of the Spuzzum area, recalled a favourite chowder or vegetable soup made by boiling salmon heads with Bitter-roots, Saskatoon Berries, Bugleweed roots, "Indian Rice", powdered Bracken Fern rhizomes, chopped wild onion and Tiger Lily bulbs.

Some Secwepemc people believed Tiger Lily bulbs to be a good health food, improving general weakness and giving one a healthier, longer life if taken in small doses.

Ktunaxa people also ate the bulbs of the Wood Lily when available.

False Solomon's Seal   *Smilacina racemosa* (L.) Desf.
Star-flowered Solomon's Seal   *S. stellata* (L.) Desf.
(Lily Family)   (Liliaceae)

Botanical Description
False Solomon's Seal is a tall perennial with a stout, fleshy rootstock and leafy, arching stems, usually growing in clumps. Broad, elliptical leaves alternate along the stem in two rows; they range from 5 to 15 cm in length, and are conspicuously parallel-veined and clasping. The flowers, small and cream-coloured, are borne in a terminal cluster. The fruits are numerous small, seedy berries growing in tight clusters; when immature, they are mottled green and brown; and when ripe they are red. Star-flowered Solomon's Seal is similar in form, but generally smaller and more slender, with fewer leaves and flowers. It produces only two to eight berries, which are larger and green with red stripes when unripe, eventually turning red. Some botanists include these species in the genus *Maianthemum.*

False Solomon's Seal.

Habitat: damp woods and open places.

Distribution in British Columbia: Star-flowered Solomon's Seal occurs throughout the province, and False Solomon's Seal is restricted to south of latitude 56°N; neither grows on Haida Gwaii.

Aboriginal Use
The Nlaka'pamux, Lower Stl'atl'imx, Secwepemc, Okanagan and Carrier ate the ripe berries of both species raw; the more northerly peoples probably ate them as well. But the Ktunaxa considered them the "Grizzly Bear's favourite food", not fit for humans. Solomon's Seal berries, though seedy, are extremely sweet, like saccharin or syrup. In

Carrier territory, False Solomon's Seal is known locally as "sugarberry". The Carrier note that bears like this berry best of all, and that it was also eaten by many smaller animals. Sekani people sometimes use the berries as a sweetener. The Okanagan used the rhizomes to flavour Black Tree Lichen and other foods in cooking-pits, and sometimes ate them alone raw. They were said to resemble onions.

Cat-tail
(Cat-tail Family)

Typha latifolia L.
(Typhaceae)

Other Names: Bulrush (this name also applies to various species of *Scirpus* in the sedge family).

Botanical Description
Cat-tail is a tall perennial with thick white fleshy rhizomes and long sword-like leaves that are greyish-green and usually 1 to 2 cm broad.

The flowers are contained in a compact brown spike, familiar to almost everyone as the cat's tail. Pollen is produced in a thinner spike immediately above the brown portion. The mature fruits are released in late summer and fall, and the cat's tail becomes a mass of greyish fuzz that is gradually blown away by the wind.

Habitat: shallow marshes, swamps and lake edges, often forming extensive pure stands.

Distribution in British Columbia: throughout the province, except on the central and northern coast, and recently introduced to Haida Gwaii; most common around pools and lakes of the southern interior.

Aboriginal Use

First Peoples in many parts of North America ate the cat-tail's starchy rhizomes, leaf bases and young flower spikes. The Okanagan, Nlaka'pamux and Lower Stl'atl'imx dug up the long, white rhizomes in early spring, claiming that they were one of the most delicious spring-time foods. The Okanagan and Nlaka'pamux cooked them in steaming pits; the Lower Stl'a-tl'imx placed them in a hot fire until the outer skin burned away, then peeled off the inner skin and ate the centre portion. The Okanagan and Carrier peeled the white lower stem and leaf bases, and ate them raw. Sekani people also ate the starch from the rhizomes, at least in this century.

Cat-tail rhizomes.

FLOWERING PLANTS
(Angiospermae)
DICOTYLEDONS

Cow Parsnip	*Heracleum lanatum* **Michx.**
(Celery Family)	**(Apiaceae or Umbelliferae)**

Other Names: "Indian Rhubarb", "Wild Rhubarb".

Botanical Description

A robust, hollow-stemmed perennial, Cow Parsnip grows 1 to 2 metres tall from a stout tap root or root cluster. The leaves are broad, and com-

pound in three large segments (one terminal and two lateral), coarsely toothed and lobed. The flowers are small, white and numerous, arranged in large flat-topped umbrella-like clusters. The leaf stems are conspicuously winged at the base. The plants have a pungent odour, especially when mature.

Habitat: moist open areas, roadsides and meadows, from sea level to above the timberline in the mountains, often in large patches.

Distribution in British Columbia: throughout the province; common in the north. The Parsnip River, a tributary of the Peace, is named after it.

Aboriginal Use

People of every aboriginal group in British Columbia used Cow Parsnip as a green vegetable. They picked the young stalks and leaf stems in spring, before the plants flowered. Then they peeled and ate them raw, or occasionally boiled, steamed or roasted them for a short while. Despite the plant's strong odour, the peeled stems are sweet and succulent, having a flavour reminiscent of celery and a texture like that of rhubarb. Some aboriginal people say that the plants in certain localities taste better than those in others.

Cow Parsnip stalks.

Some groups, notably the Stl'atl'imx, make a special distinction between the leaf stems and the bud stems. The thin and solid leaf stems ("female" stalks) they called "woman's foot"; they peeled them by splitting the fibrous skin down one side with the thumb nail, bending it back at the top, holding it with the teeth and pulling the succulent central portion away from it. The thicker, hollow bud stems ("male" stalks) they called "man's foot", and peeled them with the fingers by pulling the skin off from top to bottom in several strips.

The late Selina Timoyakin, an Okanagan elder from Penticton, recalled her family going out on Sunday picnics to gather and eat this "rhubarb". Many people still eat it today, but only casually. Some people freeze it, jar it or dehydrate it. Cow Parsnip is good dipped in sugar and served as a snack. The coastal people eat it with Eulachon grease and fish, or even with Mountain Goat head-cheese. It can also be cut in pieces, boiled, and served hot as part of a meal, and can substitute for celery in any number of dishes.

Warning

Several members of the celery family, including Water Hemlock (*Cicuta douglasii*) and Poison Hemlock (*Conium maculatum*) are violently poisonous. These plants are more slender than Cow Parsnip and have smaller flower heads and finely divided leaves. Still, it is possible to confuse these species with Cow Parsnip, especially for inexperienced observers in the spring before the plant is fully developed. Cow Parsnip and its relatives contain phototoxic compounds, which make the skin sensitive to sunlight, so they must be handled very carefully. This is why the stalks must be peeled before eating. Even lightly touching your skin to the hairs on the leaves and then exposing it to sunlight can cause blistering and discoloration that may remain for weeks or even months; the effects can be especially severe for light-skinned people. (See Turner and Szczawinski 1991 in References.)

Canby's Lovage (Celery Family)

Ligusticum canbyi Coult. & Rose (Apiaceae or Umbelliferae)

Other Names: "Indian Marijuana", "Wild Ginseng", "Wild Licorice".

Botanical Description
Canby's Lovage is a tall perennial that grows up to 120 cm tall from a thick fibrous rootstock, which is characteristically hairy, with dark stiff upright bristles around the top. The leaves, mostly basal, are compound and finely dissected. Numerous small, white flowers grow in flat-topped umbrella-like clusters, much like those of Cow Parsnip, but smaller and finer.

Habitat: moist or wet stream banks and meadows at moderate to high elevations.

Distribution in British Columbia: in the Kootenay District of the southeast; common around Kootenay Lake, Rossland and Mount Revelstoke. Also found in eastern Washington, northern Idaho and northwestern Montana.

Aboriginal Use
Canby's Lovage root, which has an unforgettable sweetish aroma, was a valuable smoking condiment of the Secwepemc, Ktunaxa and Southern Okanagan. A few pieces mixed with tobacco in a cigarette or pipe is said to give the smoke a pleasant menthol taste and to act as a

relaxant. It can also be held in the mouth as a snoose (chewing tobacco) to give the same effect. The Flathead Salish and Ktunaxa of Montana used the root of a related species, *L. verticillatum*, similarly, especially as a medicine; they smoked it to soothe a sore throat and made it into a tea for heart troubles. A piece of Canby's Lovage root held over a cut was said to stop the flow of blood immediately.

This plant was and still is extremely popular among aboriginal peoples. Places where it grows are kept secret, and people travel long distances to obtain it. The Blackfoot of Alberta sometimes come through the Rocky Mountains by train to purchase it from the Ktunaxa people.

Biscuitroot	*Lomatium canbyi* **Coult. & Rose,**
	L. cous **(Wats.) Coult. & Rose**
	and *L. farinosum* **(Hook.) Coult. & Rose**
(Celery Family)	**(Apiaceae or Umbelliferae)**

Other Names: Desert Parsley, Hog-fennel, Cous, "Camas".

Botanical Description
These species of *Lomatium* are low-growing perennial herbs with tap-roots that have a prominent globular thickening 2 cm or more below the surface of the ground. Most of the leaves are basal and finely dissected. The leaves of *Lomatium canbyi* and *L. cous* are finely divided into numerous small segments, whereas those of *L. farinosum* are divided into fewer long narrow segments. All three species have numerous small flowers that grow in irregular umbrella-like clusters; the flowers of *L. canbyi* and *L. farinosum* are white, and those of *L. cous* are yellow. The fruits of all three species are elliptical, flattened and winged.

Habitat: dry rocky slopes and foothills, often with sagebrush.

Distribution in British Columbia: none of these species occurs in the province – they are found in eastern Washington, central and northern Idaho, and western Montana.

Aboriginal Use

While these Biscuitroot species do not grow in British Columbia, the Canadian Okanagan and probably the Ktunaxa had access to their edible roots through trading with groups to the south. The Southern Okanagan, Flathead, Kalispel, Sahaptin, Nez Perce, Ktunaxa and other peoples of the northwestern United States commonly used Biscuitroot.

People dug up the roots along with Bitter-root in April and May, during or just after flowering. They ate them raw, boiled or pit-steamed. They also dried Biscuitroots on mats in the sun, then pounded them into flour and formed small round cakes. The dried roots could be stored for up to three years.

Lomatium cous was a principal food of the Nez Perce people, who traded it to the Flathead Salish, Kalispel and Southern Okanagan. *L. canbyi*, known as "White Camas" (in contrast to "Black Camas", a local name for Blue Camas) and *L. farinosum* ("Little White Camas") are still used by the Kalispel and Southern Okanagan. The latter is said to have a milder taste. They were often cooked and eaten with Bitter-root. British Columbia Okanagan people have heard of these roots, and some have tasted them, but few have seen the plants growing.

Biscuitroot (right) with Blue Camas bulbs (left) and Bitter-root (above) – these root vegetables were picked in Washington. (Courtesy of Mary Sandy.)

Chocolate Tips

(Celery Family)

Lomatium dissectum
(Nutt.) Math. & Const.
(Apiaceae or Umbelliferae)

Other Names: "Wild Celery", " Bitter-root".

Botanical Description

Chocolate Tips is a robust perennial, often growing a metre or more high from a large, woody taproot that branches out at ground-level. The leaves are large, especially the basal ones, and finely dissected into numerous small segments. The flowers are small and purple, clustered in large flat-topped umbrella-like heads, typical for the celery family. The fruits are elliptic and narrowly winged. *Lomatium dissectum* is also known as *Leptotaenia dissecta* and *Ferula dissecta.*

Habitat: dry rocky slopes, from sea level to moderate elevations in the mountains.

Distribution in British Columbia:

sporadic in the south, on both sides of the Cascades; common at Botanie Valley near Lytton, and in parts of the Okanagan Valley.

Aboriginal Use

The Okanagan and the Kalispel of Washington considered the mature flowers, leaves, stalks and roots of Chocolate Tips highly poisonous – the Okanagan used the roots as an insecticide and fish poison – but they ate the young shoots. They harvested them in early spring before the shoots emerged from the ground, locating them from the dead stalks of the previous year's growth. They ate the shoots raw, though according to L. Spier's report on the Southern Okanagan, only as a starvation food.

The Secwepemc ate the older shoots of Chocolate Tips, up to about 10 cm in height. They gathered them in April, peeled them, and ate the soft inner part. Both the Secwepemc and Nlaka'pamux ate the roots, especially from young plants, despite the previously stated report from the Okanagan people that they are poisonous. People dug up the roots in May, peeled, steamed and ate them fresh; sometimes they let the roots soften for a week or so, then spread them out, away from direct sunlight, to dry slowly. They threaded partially dried Chocolate Tips roots with a bone needle onto strings, just like Yellow Avalanche Lily bulbs, to be stored for later use. To use the dried roots, they soaked them in water for two nights, then steamed them. People often cooked and ate them together with Yellow Avalanche Lily bulbs. Though well-liked by some, Chocolate Tips roots had a reputation for bitterness; the Nlaka'pamux name for them means "bitter-head". Few people eat them today, but some remember their past use.

Desert Parsley

(Celery Family)

Lomatium macrocarpum (Nutt.) Coult. & Rose (Apiaceae or Umbelliferae)

Other Names: "Wild Carrot", "Indian Carrot", "Indian Sweet Potato", Hog-fennel, Biscuit-root.

Botanical Description
Desert Parsley is a low-growing herbaceous perennial with a fleshy tap-root that is up to 15 cm long and sometimes irregular in thickness. The

leaves, clustered near the ground, are finely dissected, and bluish-green or greyish. The flowers are white, in irregular umbrella-like clusters. The fruits are narrow, oblong to elliptic, and conspicuously winged.

Habitat: open rocky hills and plains, commonly with sagebrush.

Distribution in British Columbia: common in the dry plains and valleys of the southern interior, from Lytton eastward.

Aboriginal Use

The Nlaka'pamux, Stl'atl'imx, Secwepemc and Okanagan ate the long taproots of Desert Parsley, as did the Southern Okanagan and Kalispel in Washington. They dug up the carrot-like roots in the spring, around the time of the Bitter-root harvest. People only dug up the non-flowering, "female" plants; they said that the "male" plants with flowers or fruits were too bitter. Even the roots of the female plants are strong tasting and peppery, with a flavour akin to that of celery leaves, lingering in the mouth for a long time. Desert Parsley roots could be eaten raw, but most people roasted or boiled them, often with other foods. Nlaka'pamux people cooked them with meat or with Tiger Lily bulbs and fermented salmon roe. Some Secwepemc people sprinkled them on dried salmon heated over an open fire with dried bread. The Kalispel people of Washington called Desert Parsley roots "Indian Sweet Potatoes", which was the same name they used for commercial sweet potatoes.

According to Interior Salish tradition, the Desert Parsley root, called *qw'eqw'ila* in Secwepemc and Stl'atl'imx, was the father of a well-known mythical figure of the same name. There are many stories involving *Qw'eqw'ila* in Salish mythology. According to one Secwepemc tradition, the meadowlark sings, "don't spoil my *qw'eqw'ila*!"

Desert Parsley roots.

"Indian Celery"

Narrow-leaved Desert Parsley

Sevale Desert Parsley

(Celery Family)

Lomatium nudicaule
(Pursh) Coult. & Rose
L. triternatum
(Pursh) Coult. & Rose
L. ambiguum
(Nutt.) Coult. & Rose
(Apiaceae or Umbelliferae)

Other Names: "Wild Celery" (all); "Indian Consumption Plant", Bare-stem Lomatium (*L. nudicaule*); Desert Parsley (*L. ambiguum*).

Botanical Description
These *Lomatium* species are herbaceous perennials with a solitary stem or clustered stems growing from a stout taproot. "Indian Celery" is usually 20 to 60 cm tall. The leaves are thick, bluish-green and compound, divided into 3 to 30 oval to lance-shaped leaflets, which may or may not be toothed at the tips. The flowers are light yellow, small, and numerous, in loose umbrella-like clusters with rays of varying lengths. The fruits are oblong or elliptical, winged and flattened. Narrow-leaved Desert Parsley is similar to "Indian Celery", but with narrower leaf segments, in some varieties only 1 or 2 mm wide. Sevale Desert Parsley is shorter, it has narrow, usually unequal leaf segments, and its taproot is irregularly shaped with tuberous lumps between narrow segments. The flowers of Narrow-leaved and Sevale desert parsleys are a darker shade of yellow than those of "Indian Celery". *Lomatium nudicaule* is also known as *L. leiocarpum.*

Habitat: dry open slopes, meadows and sparsely wooded places from valleys and foothills to moderate elevations in the mountains.

Distribution in British Columbia: confined to dry areas in the south; "Indian Celery" is found both west and east of the Cascades, and is common on Vancouver Island and the Gulf Islands as well as at Botanie Valley, Pemberton and many other interior locations; the other two species are found only in the southern interior.

Aboriginal Use

The young sprouts, leaf-stalks and leaves of "Indian Celery" were a popular green vegetable of the Nlaka'pamux, Stl'atl'imx and Secwepemc. People gathered the greens from April to June, up to the time the flowers finished blooming, and ate them raw or boiled. The Stl'atl'imx of the Pemberton area used to let them sit overnight after boiling, then feed them to children as a special treat. Some Stl'atl'imx and Nlaka'pamux people still gather them and preserve them by freezing or canning. "Indian Celery" greens have a strong but pleasant flavour, like celery leaves. The Nlaka'pamux also used to eat the young roots of "Indian Celery", but not after 1920, according to James Teit's notes.

"Indian Celery".

Interior Salish peoples used the flowers, leaves, stems and seeds of all three species as flavouring for teas, soups, meat stews and tobacco. To make tea, a person put the plants, fresh or dried, in water and brought it to a boil. "Indian Celery" tea is said to be a good tonic for colds and sore throats – the Nlaka'pamux used it often. The Coast Salish of Vancouver Island and Puget Sound considered "Indian Celery" seeds a valuable cold medicine. Sometimes, Secwepemc and Okanagan people added the plants to steaming-pits to flavour roots, and even today they cook them in soups and meat dishes. The Stl'atl'imx, and probably other groups as well, mixed the dried seeds with tobacco in pipes or cigarettes to give it a menthol taste.

Sevale Desert Parsley.

Sweet Cicely
(Celery Family)

Osmorhiza berteroi DC.
(Apiaceae or Umbelliferae)

Other Names: Sweet Root, "Dry-land Parsnip".

Botanical Description
Sweet Cicely is a perennial herb with a well-developed taproot. The stems, solitary or clustered, are slender and up to a metre high when flowering or fruiting. The leaves are compound, with oval, notched

leaflets 2 to 7 cm long and usually coarsely toothed. The basal leaves are long stemmed, and the plants have a loose, bushy appearance. The small, white flowers grow in irregular umbrella-like clusters, with few flowers in a cluster. The fruits are black and needle-like, often catching in one's clothing. *Osmorhiza berteroi* is also known as *O. chilensis*.

Habitat: partially shaded woodlands, from sea level to moderate elevations in the mountains.

Distribution in British Columbia: along the entire coast, and throughout the central and southern interior.

Aboriginal Use
The Nlaka'pamux and Lower Stl'atl'imx ate the thick aromatic roots of Sweet Cicely. They dug them up in March and April, and either steamed them in underground pits (if they could gather enough) or boiled them in stews with salmon eggs or meat. Sweet Cicely roots were known for their delicate sweet flavour. The Pemberton Stl'atl'imx called them "Dry-land Parsnips" to distinguish them from Water Parsnips.

Warning
At some stages, Sweet Cicely resembles Water Hemlock (*Cicuta douglasii*) and Poison Hemlock (*Conium maculatum*) – see the Warning under Cow Parsnip, on page 79. Before you taste any wild plant in the celery family, be absolutely sure of its identity.

Wild Caraway

(Celery Family)

Perideridia gairdneri (H. & A.) Mathias (Apiaceae or Umbelliferae)

Other Names: Gairdner's Yampah, False Caraway, "Indian Carrot", "Wild Carrot".

Botanical Description
Wild Caraway is a slender perennial that grows 50 cm or more tall from a single or bifurcated spindle-shaped root, which is about as thick as one's finger and several centimetres long. The leaves are compound, with very narrow segments, usually withering before the plant blooms; their grass-like appearance makes this plant easy to overlook unless it is in full flower. The flowers are small and white, and grow in umbrella-like clusters.

Habitat: dry to moist open woods and meadows, from lowlands to moderate elevations.

Distribution in British Columbia:
throughout the south; its populations are often scattered, but may be common in some localities.

Aboriginal Use
The Okanagan and Ktunaxa, and possibly other interior peoples, ate the sweet, anise-flavoured roots of Wild Caraway, as did the Southern Okanagan, Kalispel, Flathead and other groups in Washington, Idaho and Montana. Lewis and Clark, the well-known naturalist-explorers, were introduced to this root by several aboriginal groups during their travels and found it to be a pleasant, palatable food, either roasted, boiled or dried.

Aboriginal people dug up Wild Caraway roots in May and June, at the same time as Bitter-root, and ate them raw, boiled or pit-steamed. Sometimes they dried the cooked roots and mixed them with powdered deer meat as a special treat. The Southern Okanagan used to boil them with Saskatoon Berries, Black Tree Lichen, or more recently, flour, to make a thick pudding. Raw Wild Caraway roots could be stored for winter by packing them in an earth pit lined with pine needles or cottonwood bark to protect them from frost and rodents. Few people still use the roots today, but many of those who ate them as children remember them fondly.

Water Parsnip *Sium suave* Walt.
(Celery Family) (Apiaceae or Umbelliferae)

Other Names: "Swamp Parsnip", "Wild Swamp Carrot", "Wild Saccharin".

Botanical Description
Water Parsnip is a perennial herb, 50 to 120 cm tall, with stout strongly ribbed stems and fibrous roots, often originating from the lower nodes of the stem. A cluster of long, fleshy roots resembling miniature parsnips grows at the base of the stem. The leaves are singly compound,

with 7 to 13 narrow, finely toothed leaflets, each attached directly to the central stalk in a feather-like fashion. The flowers are small and white, in dense umbrella-like heads.

Habitat: swampy places and shallow water around the edges of lakes and ponds.

Distribution in British Columbia: common throughout the province, except on Haida Gwaii.

Aboriginal Use
The Okanagan, Secwepemc, Nlaka'pamux, Lower Stl'atl'imx, Carrier, Ktunaxa and probably other interior peoples ate the sweet, finger-like roots of Water Parsnip, as did some coastal groups. J.J. Honigmann, in *Ethnography and Acculturation of the Fort Nelson Slave* (1946), reported that a certain "Wild Carrot", undoubtedly this species, grew in the Fort Nelson area, being particularly abundant along the Deer River, and

that the Dene-thah people often lived on them in times of famine. Water Parsnips were probably eaten by other northern Athapaskan groups as well.

People dug up the roots in spring and early summer, washed and ate them raw or steamed. The raw roots are crisp and delicious with a definite carroty flavour; some Ktunaxa people call them "Wild Saccharin". Sometimes, people ate the young green shoots, but the older plants were not edible; some Secwepemc people considered the flowers poisonous. Cattle often eat the leaves and stems.

The Secwepemc used to dig the roots in the wet meadows around Kamloops and Shuswap Lake. The Nlaka'pamux got them at Nicola and Coldwater lakes, and the Ktunaxa at Bains Lake.

Warning
Water Parsnip has been implicated in numerous cases of livestock poisoning, although according to Kingsbury (1964), these cases are not entirely convincing. Judging from their use by British Columbian First Peoples, the roots and young stems are not poisonous, but the flower-tops may be. Water Parsnip often grows with Water Hemlock (*Cicuta douglasii*), which is violently poisonous, and the danger of confusing these two species is serious indeed, since they closely resemble each other. The leaves of Water Hemlock are three-times compound (the leaflets are not in a simple feather-like arrangement) while Water Parsnip leaves are only once compound (the leaflets are all attached directly to the central leaf stalk). Water Hemlock also has a distinctive chambered turnip-like swelling at the base of the stem, which is absent in Water Parsnip. If you are even slightly uncertain about identifying a Water Parsnip plant, leave it alone.

Balsamroot
(Aster Family)

Balsamorhiza sagittata (Pursh) Nutt.
(Asteraceae or Compositae)

Other Names: Spring Sunflower, "Wild Sunflower".

Botanical Description
Balsamroot is a perennial that grows 30 to 45 cm high from a thick deep-seated taproot. It has numerous large long-stemmed leaves that grow in clusters; they are shaped like arrow heads and appear grey or silvery because of a thick covering of fine white hairs. The flower heads, usually many per plant, are borne on individual stems and are bright yellow, resembling small sunflowers, with about 25 petal-like ray flowers per head. The fruits, which shake loose easily from the mature dried flower heads, are like miniature sunflower seeds. Blooming season is from April to July, depending on elevation, at which time these plants provide a striking display of colour on the hillsides and valleys of the southern interior.

Habitat: open dry hillsides and flats, from lowlands to moderate elevations in the mountains.

Distribution in British Columbia: widespread and abundant throughout the drier regions of the southern interior.

Aboriginal Use

Balsamroot certainly ranks among the most versatile food plants used by the peoples of the southern interior. The roots, young shoots, bud-stems and seeds were all popular foods. All of the Interior Salish groups ate them, as did the Tsilhqot'in and Ktunaxa peoples.

Balsamroots.

In early spring, from March to April, just as Balsamroot leaves began to show above the ground, people dug up the taproots. Although the taproots grow more than 30 cm long and 8 cm across, people usually selected the smaller, carrot-sized roots. They could be dug up later in the season, but the roots become stringy and tough in summer. To prepare the roots, a person beat them to loosen the tough outer skin, then peeled them and steamed the whitish inner part overnight. The cooked roots are brownish, with a sweetish taste. They could be eaten immediately; or they could be threaded on a string or skewered on a stick, then dried. Many people regarded cooked Balsamroots as a treat or dessert. Nowadays, people bake them in ovens or steam them on top of the stove and serve them hot as a vegetable. The roots contain inulin, a complex and somewhat indigestible carbohydrate; pit-steaming partially breaks down the inulin into units of fructose, an easily digested sugar.

Even before the roots were ready to be dug, people sought out the whitish succulent shoots, before they appeared above the ground. They located the shoots from the dead leaves and flower stalks of the previous year's growth, dug them up and ate them raw. Balsamroot shoots were a good famine food, being available when few other foods could be found.

In April and May, when the flower buds were still tightly closed, people gathered the bud stems, peeled them, and ate them raw, steamed or boiled. They have a pleasant nutty taste, reminiscent of the smell of young sunflower seeds. Some people also peeled and ate the young leaf stalks.

Balsamroot seeds.

After the flowers had withered and gone to seed, people collected the small black seeds, shaking them from the dried heads. Sometimes, they spread the seeds in the sun or roasted them, then ate them whole; more often, they placed the seeds in a basket or buckskin bag and pounded them into a meal. They ate this meal alone, without further preparation, or combined it with powdered Saskatoon Berries and a little sugar, and ate the mixture with spoons; they might also mix the meal with deer fat or grease and water, boil it and form it into small cakes. Properly dried seeds would last up to six years, if stored in air-tight containers. Their flavour resembles that of cultivated sunflower seeds. Balsamroot seeds are seldom eaten today.

One Ktunaxa man noted that horses like to eat the Balsamroot plant as a "dessert" – you can smell it on their breath when they eat it.

Okanagan, Sahaptin and other interior peoples of Washington ate the roots of other *Balsamorhiza* species, but as far as we know, British Columbia's coastal species, *B. deltoidea*, which grows from southern Vancouver Island to southern California, was not used similarly by the Coast Salish. The Flathead Salish of Montana, and possibly also the Ktunaxa of Montana and British Columbia, ate the roots of a similar plant, known as Mule's Ears.

Wild Thistles:

Edible Thistle	*Cirsium edule* **Nutt.**
Hooker's Thistle	*C. hookerianum* **Nutt.**
Wavy-leaved Thistle	*C. undulatum* **(Nutt.) Spreng.**
(Aster Family)	**(Asteraceae or Compositae)**

Other Names: Indian Thistle; Mountain Thistle (*Cirsium edule*); Woolly Thistle (*C. undulatum*).

Botanical Description

Wild thistles are tap-rooted biennials or short-lived perennials, forming a basal rosette of prickly leaves during the first year and flowering on the second or succeeding years; Edible Thistle reputedly flowers only once. The flowering stalks are usually 1 to 1.5 metres high, with scattered spiny leaves that gradually diminish in size toward the top. The large flower heads are borne singly or in loose terminal clusters. Edible Thistle has moderately spiny greenish leaves and flower heads – especially the buds – which are covered with long, white hairs, like dense cobwebbing. The flowers are bright reddish purple. Hook-er's Thistle has similar leaves and flower

Wavy-leaved Thistle.

heads, but has creamy white flowers. The leaves of Wavy-leaved Thistle are silvery grey, strongly lobed and very spiny; the flower heads are also spiny and have pale pink-purple flowers.

Habitat: Edible Thistle grows in wet meadows and moist open woods, chiefly in the mountains; Hooker's Thistle is found in moist bottom-lands and on open rocky slopes; and Wavy-leaved Thistle grows in dry well-drained open places in foothills and plains.

Distribution in British Columbia: Edible Thistle occurs in the Coast and Cascade mountains from northern British Columbia southward; Hooker's Thistle occurs mainly in the montane areas and plains in the

central and southeastern part of the province; and Wavy-leaved Thistle is found in the dry areas of the southern interior.

Aboriginal Use
These species, like Indian Thistle on the coast (*Cirsium brevistylum*), have edible tap roots, which were used by some aboriginal peoples. The Nlaka'pamux ate the roots of all three species, but only those of the first-year non-flowering plants. People gathered the roots in fall, peeled, cut up, and steamed them in pits, or boiled them in stews. When raw, wild thistle roots resemble white carrots, but after cooking they turn brown. They are said to taste like Balsamroot roots. Many people believed that wild thistle roots were nutritious and a good health food, but would give you gas if you ate too many. Like Balsamroot, thistles contain inulin, the complex and somewhat indigestible sugar, and are known to cause flatulence. The Secwepemc ate the roots of Wavy-leaved Thistle, and the Flathead Salish of Montana ate the roots and succulent young stalks of Hooker's Thistle, but the Stl'atl'imx, Okanagan, Ktunaxa and Athapaskan peoples apparently did not recognize them as a food. The Stl'atl'imx used the root of Wavy-leaved Thistle as a pain-killer for a toothache, applying a piece of boiled root directly on the affected tooth.

Hooker's Thistle.

Hawkweeds   *Hieracium* spp.
Mountain Dandelions   *Agoseris* spp.
Other Latex-producing Plants
(Aster Family)   (Asteraceae or Compositae)

Botanical Description
Hawkweeds are slender, fibrous-rooted perennial herbs with smooth-edged or toothed leaves all basal or alternating along the stem, the largest toward the bottom. The leaves are often covered with short, stiff bristles, which make them prickly to touch. The flowers, resembling

miniature dandelion heads, are borne terminally in loose clusters; in native species, they range in colour from creamy white to yellow. Mountain Dandelions, as the name implies, are similar to a Common Dandelion: they have a taproot and a cluster of narrow, smooth-edged or slightly lobed basal leaves; they produce a solitary yellow or orange dandelion-sized flower, and later, a round parachute-covered seed head. When cut or crushed, the leaves, stems and roots of Hawkweeds and Mountain Dandelions exude a milky, bitter-tasting latex that darkens and coagulates on exposure to the air.

Mountain Dandelion (*Agoseris glauca*).

Habitat: Hawkweeds are found in a variety of habitats, mostly in dry open areas, from lowlands to moderate or high elevations; Mountain Dandelions are found in open meadows and woodlands from valley bottoms to mountain slopes.

Distribution in British Columbia: at least seven species of Hawkweed and four of Mountain Dandelion are found in the province.

Aboriginal Use

According to James Teit (see Steedman 1930 in References), the Nlaka'pamux chewed the leaves and coagulated latex of two or three species of Hawkweed (probably *Hieracium albertinum, H. cynoglossoides* and *H. scouleri*), at least one species of Mountain Dandelion (*Agoseris glauca*) and an introduced species, Salsify. The Nlaka'pamux broke the leaves and stems of these plants, allowing the milky latex to ooze out. When the latex hardened, they rolled it in a little ball and chewed it for pleasure and to cleanse the mouth, swallowing it afterward. The Okanagan, Spokane, and Kalispel chewed the latex of *A. glauca* var. *dasycephala*. The Spokane call it "Indian bubble gum". They often dried the leaves, then chewed them to extract the gum. The Okanagan, Secwepemc, Flathead and perhaps some other groups chewed the latex of Milkweed in a similar manner.

Oregon Grape

(Barberry Family)

Mahonia aquifolium (Pursh) Nutt. and *M. nervosa* (Pursh) Nutt. (Berberidaceae)

Other Names: Barberry, Mahonia; Tall Oregon Grape, Tall Mahonia (*M. aquifolium*); Dull Oregon Grape (*M. nervosa*).

Botanical Description

These species of Oregon Grape are low shrubs with leathery holly-like compound leaves, elongated clusters of bright yellow flowers, and long

clusters of round, deep-blue berries that have a greyish waxy coating. The bark is light yellow-grey outside and bright yellow inside. *Mahonia aquifolium* is the tallest, sometimes exceeding 2 metres, with 5 to 7 leaflets per leaf. *M. nervosa* has usually 9 to 15 leaflets. Some botanists include these species in the genus *Berberis*. A short subspecies of *M. aquifolium* is sometimes called Creeping Oregon Grape (ssp. *repens*).

Habitat: *M. aquifolium* grows in dry open rocky areas, whereas *M. nervosa* prefers light to shaded coniferous forest.

Distribution in British Columbia: *M. aquifolium* occurs throughout the southern part of the province; *M. nervosa* is confined to the southern coastal forests west of the Cascade Mountains.

Aboriginal Use

The Nlaka'pamux, Stl'atl'imx, Okanagan, Secwepemc, Ktunaxa and Carrier ate the tart berries of Oregon Grape, as did several coastal groups. All interior groups ate the fruit of *M. aquifolium*, whereas only the Lower Nlaka'pamux and Lower Stl'atl'imx had access to *M. nervosa* berries. They gathered the berries in mid August, when fully ripe. The

Southern Okanagan of Washington used to mash and dry them in cakes, but most groups simply ate them fresh. Nowadays they are canned or made into a tangy and delicious jelly. Oregon Grape, especially the bark and wood, was well known among the First Peoples of British Columbia as a tonic and blood purifier. Some people believed that eating the berries was healthful and beneficial to the blood.

In his "Notes Archaeological, Industrial, and Sociological on the Western Dénés" (1893), Father Morice records that the Carrier once ate not only the berries but the young leaves of *M. aquifolium*, simmering them in a small amount of water until they were tender.

Hazelnut	***Corylus cornuta* Marsh.**
(Birch Family)	**(Betulaceae)**

Other Names: Wild Filbert, Cobnut.

Botanical Description
Hazelnut is a bushy shrub, usually 2 to 5 metres tall, spreading and profusely branching. The young twigs are woolly. The leaves are broadly oval, pointed and sharply toothed. The male flowers are long, yellowish catkins, maturing in early spring. The nuts grow singly or in clusters of two or three at the ends of the twigs. They are encased in long tubular light-green husks, covered with prickly hairs. When ripe, the nuts resemble commercial filberts.

Habitat: from shaded forests on the coast to open rocky slopes in the interior.

Distribution in British Columbia: widespread throughout the southern part of the province from Vancouver Island to the Kootenays, and extending into the northern interior as far as the Nass and Skeena rivers.

Aboriginal Use

The Nlaka'pamux, Stl'atl'imx, Okanagan, Secwepemc, Ktunaxa, Nisga'a, Gitxsan and Wet'suwet'en ate Hazelnuts whenever they could find them. They usually gathered the nuts in October and buried them in the ground for ten days or more to allow the prickly husks to rot away. Sometimes they hastened this process by adding water to the hole before filling it in and by covering the nuts with wet mud. After removing the husks, they shelled the nuts and ate them. An easier way to obtain the nuts was to locate them, already dehusked, in squirrels' caches. The Nlaka'pamux used to crack small quantities of the nuts by placing them in their moccasins and running on them, a procedure recommended only for those with tough feet! (The photograph on page 26 shows Hazelnuts with and without husks.)

The Lakes people made a special type of "relish" with hazelnuts. They crushed the nuts and mixed them with bear fat and sometimes berries and meat, then formed the mixture into cakes to dry or stuffed it into an animal intestine (like a sausage) for storage.

Hazelnuts were widely traded among the aboriginal groups of the province. The Stl'atl'imx obtained them from the Halkomelem at Agassiz and from the Secwepemc at Quesnel. The Lower Nlaka'pamux also bought them from the Halkomelem and from the Upper Nlaka'pamux, who gathered them in large numbers and traded them also to the Secwepemc, especially during annual tribal gatherings at Green Lake near Clinton. Bears and squirrels are as fond of the nuts as humans are. Today, children still go out to gather them, but they have for the most part been replaced by commercial nuts, such as peanuts.

Brittle Prickly-pear
Plains Prickly-pear
(Cactus Family)

Opuntia fragilis (Nutt.) Haw.
O. polyacantha Haw.
(Cactaceae)

Botanical Description
These prickly-pears are low-growing perennials, often spreading into mats several metres broad. They have jointed succulent stems covered with clusters of a few rigid long spines, up to 5 cm long, arising from cushions of numerous short bristles. The flowers are 5 to 7 cm long, yellow, sometimes turning pinkish with age, with many petals and stamens, and very showy. The fruits are small, berry-like, reddish and spiny. The stem segments of Brittle Prickly-pear are round in cross-section and usually 2 to 5 cm long, whereas those of Plains Prickly-pear are strongly flattened and mostly 5 to 15 cm long.

Habitat: dry hillsides and open plains.

Distribution in British Columbia: common in the dry valleys and hills of the southern interior; Brittle Prickly-pear extends north into the Peace River region and also occurs on the rocky points of southern Vancouver Island and the Gulf Islands.

Brittle Prickly-pear (below)
and Plains Prickly-pear (right).

Aboriginal Use

Despite their formidable spines, the succulent stem segments of prickly-pears were an important food of the Interior Salish. People usually gathered them in the spring; but in times of necessity in mid winter, they would dig them out from under the snow. They scorched off the spines in a hot fire, then roasted or pit-cooked the segments, peeled them and ate the inner fleshy part. Some people, instead of peeling them, simply squeezed the cooked segments, and the edible inner part popped out, just like the inside of a cooked marshmallow. People also ate the fruits, though they are small and dry in comparison to the fruits of larger prickly-pears in the southwestern United States. The Okanagan used to cook cactus flesh in soup, or mix it with deer fat. The Nlaka'pamux mixed it with berries, and some people have recently used it as an ingredient in fruit cakes. It may be preserved by canning in fruit juice. In the Okanagan area, the blooming of the prickly-pears in June and July is an indicator that the Saskatoon Berries are ready to be picked.

Blue Elderberry.

Red Elderberry.

Blue Elderberry
Red Elderberry
(Honeysuckle Family)

Sambucus cerulea Raf.
S. racemosa L.
(Caprifoliaceae)

Botanical Description
Elderberries are large, bushy shrubs, sometimes tree-like, 2 to 5 metres tall, with brittle, pith-filled branches and grey-brown bark. The leaves are large and pinnately compound, each bearing five to nine pointed oval leaflets. The flowers are small and creamy-white. Blue Elderberry flowers are crowded in large flat-topped clusters, whereas Red Elderberry's flower clusters are smaller and pyramidal. Both species produce numerous small, seedy fruits. Those of Blue Elderberry are dark blue, appearing powder-blue due to a whitish waxy coating; the fruits of Red Elderberry are bright red (or black in one form). *Sambucus cerulea* is also known as *S. glauca*, and *S. racemosa* is also called *S. pubens*.

Habitat: Blue Elderberry grows in valley bottoms and in gulleys on open dry slopes, and Red Elderberry occurs in open swampy areas, moist clearings and shaded forests; both are found from sea level to moderate elevations.

Distribution in British Columbia: Blue Elderberry is common in the southern interior, in the Okanagan and Columbia River valleys, and sporadic on southern Vancouver Island and the Gulf Islands; Red Elderberry is widespread along the coast, extending into the interior along major river valleys, and recurring in the interior wet belt along the Columbia River, where its dark-colour form is common.

Aboriginal Use
The use of elderberries by indigenous peoples reflects the ranges of these species in the province. Most coastal First Peoples ate Red Elderberries, but only a few groups had access to Blue Elderberries. On the other hand, most southern interior groups harvested Blue Elderberries, and Red Elderberries were used only by the transitional groups of the Cascade and Coast mountains – the Lower Nlaka'pamux, Lower Stl'atl'imx, Nisga'a and Gitxsan – and the Ktunaxa.

The Nlaka'pamux, Stl'atl'imx, Secwepemc, Okanagan and Ktunaxa gathered Blue Elderberries in late summer. The Nlaka'pamux, especially, ate large quantities of the fresh berries and dried much of the fruit for winter use. The Okanagan ate few fresh berries but stored large numbers for winter use by a rather unusual procedure. They left the berries hanging on the bushes until November, just before the first snow, then harvested them in bunches. Clearing the ground around the base of a Ponderosa Pine, they spread a layer of pine needles on the earth, then laid the bunches of elderberries stems up on the needles. After this, they placed a thick layer of pine needles over the top. Soon after, a layer of insulating snow would cover the berries. Throughout the winter, the Okanagan people dug up clusters of the berries and ate them, but not too many at a time – "just enough to get a taste". These caches of elderberries were easy be locate, because the fruit coloured the snow above them a bluish-pink. Occasionally, the Okanagan steamed Black Tree Lichen together with elderberries to flavour it. Nowadays they and other aboriginal people use the berries to make preserves and syrup.

The interior groups that used Red Elderberries prepared them in the same way the coastal peoples did, by steaming or boiling. Some Nla-ka'pamux people flavoured salmon by soaking it in Red Elderberry juice overnight before baking it. Salmon prepared in this way was said to have an excellent taste.

High-bush Cranberries: *Viburnum edule* (left) and *V. opulus* (below).

High-bush Cranberry

(Honeysuckle Family)

Viburnum edule (Michx.) Raf. and *V. opulus* L. (Caprifoliaceae)

Other Name: Squashberry (*V. edule*); Moosewood (*V. opulus*).

Botanical Description
These species of High-bush Cranberry are straggling shrubs, 50 to 250 cm high, with smooth reddish bark. The leaves of *Viburnum edule* are opposite and shallowly three-lobed or occasionally lobeless; those of *V. opulus* are also opposite but more deeply three-lobed. The flowers of *V. edule* are borne in small rounded clusters; the flower clusters of *V. opulus* are larger and showier. The fruits of both species are round, shiny and red to orange. When unripe they are hard and extremely acidic; later, especially after a frost, they become soft and palatable, though tart. Each berry contains a large, flattened seed. *V. edule* is also known as *V. pauciflorum*, and *V. opulus* is also known as *V. trilobum*.

Habitat: moist woods and stream-banks, from near sea level to moderate elevations in the mountains.

Distribution in British Columbia: *V. edule* is found throughout the province from sea level to subalpine forests; *V. opulus* grows in the interior wet belt, in the North Thompson, Columbia and Kootenay river valleys.

Aboriginal Use
All interior aboriginal groups used *V. edule* fruits wherever they were available. The Secwepemc and Ktunaxa were the only groups with access to *V. opulus* berries.

People usually harvested the tart berries in late fall, after they had been softened and sweetened by the frost. They picked them in bunches, or if the berries were very ripe, shook them onto mats or bark trays. Some people ate them raw, chewing them, swallowing the juice and spitting out the seeds. The Nlaka'pamux named the berries for the loud clicking sound the seeds make when chewed. Carrier people sometimes ate them with bear grease. Sometimes, if High-bush Cranberries ripened early enough, they were mixed with fresh Saskatoon Berries to flavour them. Father Morice noted that the fruit was much appreciated by the Carrier people despite its pungency. People enjoy

High-bush Cranberries especially when they pick them frozen off the bushes in winter. At this time, the berries are a treat for trappers and others travelling in the woods.

The Nisga'a, following the traditions of the coastal peoples, boil the berries and mix them with oil. In winter, they sometimes make a kind of "ice cream" (not the same as the Indian ice cream made from Soapberries) by whipping them to a froth with Eulachon oil and freshly fallen snow. Today the berries are used everywhere for jams and jellies. Some Sekani people also make tea from them.

The Carrier people used to smoke the bark, but this practice was not widespread. The Secwepemc note that grouse and other birds like to eat the berries.

Red Osier Dogwood	*Cornus sericea* L.
(Dogwood Family)	(Cornaceae)

Other Names: Red-willow, Western Dogwood.

Botanical Description
A slender branching shrub, Red Osier Dogwood usually grows 2 to 3 metres tall. Its branches are opposite; their bark is often conspicuously red (but sometimes green), smooth and shiny. The leaves are oval to elliptical, smooth-edged and pointed, turning bright red in fall. The numerous flowers are small and white, and grow in flat-topped clusters. The clustered berries are pea-sized and white, often with a bluish or greenish tinge; they are fleshy and have a small, hard stone in the

centre. There are two varieties of Red Osier Dogwood: var. *stolonifera* has smooth stones and var. *occidentalis* has grooved stones. The former is more common east of the Coast Mountains, the latter west of the Coast Mountains, but they tend to intergrade. *Cornus sericea* is also known as *C. stolonifera*.

Habitat: moist soil, along streams and lake edges.

Distribution in British Columbia: widespread, from valley bottoms to near the timberline.

Aboriginal Use

Red Osier Dogwood berries are extremely bitter and many people believe them to be inedible. But they were eaten by all of the southern interior aboriginal groups, including Nlaka'pamux, Stl'atl'imx, Okanagan, Secwepemc and Ktunaxa. People gathered the berries from August to October. Most considered the pure white berries less bitter than those tinged with blue. They usually ate them fresh, often mashing them with sweeter fruits, such as Choke Cherries or Saskatoon Berries. The Ktunaxa and others made a dish called "sweet and sour", consisting of mashed Red Osier Dogwood berries, Saskatoons and a little sugar. Sometimes, people dried the berries in cakes to be mixed with dried Saskatoons later in the year. Apparently, the Lower Stl'atl'imx of Pemberton did not eat the fleshy part of the fruit, but mashed the berries and extracted the stones, which they stored and ate later, like peanuts.

Some people smoked the leaves or bark of Red Osier Dogwood, or mixed them with tobacco. The Carrier smoked the bark for sickness of the lungs. The Lower Stl'atl'imx sometimes called the fruits "bear berries" – they said that the bears come down from the mountains to get the berries at the same time that people harvest them.

Soapberry
(Oleaster Family)

Shepherdia canadensis (L.) Nutt.
(Elaeagnaceae)

Other Names: Soopolallie (Chinook jargon), Russet Buffalo-berry, Foamberry.

Botanical Description

Soapberry is a spreading to erect shrub 1 to 4 metres tall, with smooth brownish-grey bark and oval leaves usually 25 to 50 mm long. The buds, young twigs and backs of the leaves are conspicuously dotted with coppery scales. The flowers are small and inconspicuous; male and female flowers grow on separate bushes. The berries are small, slightly elongated, soft, orange-red and translucent; they have a strong sour-bitter taste.

Habitat: dry open woods.

Distribution in British Columbia: throughout the province, except in humid coastal forests; widespread in the interior, from lowlands to subalpine forests; not found on Haida Gwaii.

Aboriginal Use

As on the coast, these tart, somewhat bitter berries were widely used by interior First Peoples. Soapberries were not eaten like other fruits, but whipped with water into a light froth, often called "Indian ice cream". The berries ripen any time from May to August, depending on elevation and latitude. People usually harvest them by placing a mat, tray or bucket beneath the fruit-laden branches and whacking the branches sharply with a stick, so that the ripe berries fall onto the mat or into the container. They can separate the berries from leaves, twigs and other debris by hand or by rolling them down a slanted board into a basket or tray – everything else sticks to the board. The berries can be eaten fresh, or they can be dried for later use by boiling them and spreading them on trays or dried grass and placing them over a small fire or in a well-ventilated spot for several days. Sometimes people poured the juice obtained from boiling the Soapberries over the drying cakes a little at a time. If they dried the berries on grass (such as Bluebunch Wheatgrass or Pinegrass), they could store the cakes with the grass still stuck to them. Later, when people whipped the Soapberries into Indian ice cream, the grass helped in raising the foam; they simply scooped the grass off the top when eating the Indian ice cream. Nowadays people usually preserve Soapberries by canning or freezing.

To make Indian ice cream, add a quarter cup of water to one cup of fresh Soapberries or two tablespoons of canned or dried berries or Soapberry concentrate. Beat the mixture into a light foam, to the consistency of beaten egg whites. The traditional method is to beat Indian ice cream with the hands or with a special beater made of Rocky Mountain Maple bark or some other material; but you can use an egg-beater or electric mixer. After the foam begins to form, add sugar gradually – usually three to four tablespoons per cup of fresh berries – and continue beating until the foam is ready. You may need to add more water. Traditionally, Saskatoon Berries and other fruits were mixed in as sweeteners. The above quantities will make four to six servings. Green Soapberries will yield a white foam, while ripe berries produce a froth of a light pink or salmon colour. Take care never to allow the berries to come in contact with grease or oil, or they will not whip.

The taste of Soapberries is acquired; few people enjoy Indian ice cream the first time they try it. Even the sweetened froth has a sour-bitter taste. But once you get used to it, you may find it a novel and enjoyable treat.

As well as being a confection, Soapberries are said to be an excellent health food. People take a teaspoonful of berries and juice for ailments ranging from indigestion to the flu. The Nlaka'pamux, Stl'atl'imx and Secwepemc make a kind of "lemonade" from canned Soapberry juice,

Indian ice cream
and canned
Soapberries.

mixed with sugar and water. Not only is this drink refreshing on a hot summer's day, but it is also said to be a good cure for acne, boils, digestive troubles and even gallstones. The Secwepemc boil the twigs and sticks, alone or with Cascara bark, as a laxative.

Throughout the province, Soapberries have been a major item of trade and commerce among aboriginal peoples. In areas such as Nisga'a territory, where the plants are not common, people were able to obtain the dried berries from neighbouring groups. Today they are highly prized; people in many communities eat them on special occasions and frequently exchange them as gifts.

Crowberry
(Crowberry Family)

Empetrum nigrum L.
(Empetraceae)

Botanical Description

Crowberry is a low, spreading evergreen shrub, up to 30 cm high. The leaves are dark green and needle-like, giving the plant the appearance

of a miniature fir tree. The flowers are pinkish and inconspicuous. The berries are globular, purplish or black, and grow singly along the stem or in clusters of two to five; they are juicy, but have large hard seeds.

Habitat: swamps, muskegs and rocky mountain slopes.

Distribution in British Columbia: throughout the province.

Aboriginal Use

The Carrier, Sekani, Dene-thah and probably other Athapaskan groups ate Crowberries both fresh and dried. The Dene-thah gathered them all winter from under the snow. The Carrier sometimes mixed them with bear grease. To dry Crowberries, people mashed them, cooked them with heated stones in long spruce-bark troughs, then spread them on trays, as they did to dry Saskatoon Berries. To prepare dried Crowberries for eating, they simply soaked them in water. They taste somewhat acidic. Sekani people noted that the berries can be eaten as a thirst quencher.

Kinnikinnick (Heather Family)

Arctostaphylos uva-ursi (L.) Spreng. (Ericaceae)

Other Name: Bearberry.

Botanical Description
Kinnikinnick is a low, trailing evergreen shrub, 5 to 15 cm tall, forming a dense mat. The bark is reddish and scaly. The leaves are 15 to 30 mm long with short stems; they are thick, oblong and rounded, tapering at the base. The flowers are pink and urn-shaped, growing in small clusters. The berries are globular and bright red; the flesh is white, dry and mealy, with a hard seed inside.

Habitat: dry slopes, sand and well-drained soils in exposed areas.

Distribution in British Columbia: widespread from sea level to high elevations.

Aboriginal Use
Most interior aboriginal groups ate Kinnikinnick berries raw or cooked. The Nlaka'pamux, Stl'atl'imx, Okanagan, Secwepemc, Ktunaxa, Carrier, Wet'suwet'en, Sekani and Nisga'a gathered the berries from late summer until well into winter, and even dug them out from under the snow. According to the Okanagan, some localities yield sweet, good-tasting berries whereas others have berries with hardly any taste at all. People cooked Kinnikinnick berries by frying them in salmon oil or bear fat, or by boiling them in soups or with deer meat, Moose or salmon. The berries are too dry to eat alone. The Nisga'a boiled them and preserved them in oil, then served them during the

winter whipped with snow. The Lakes people made a special ceremonial food by mixing crushed Kinnikinnick berries with salmon eggs. Sekani people – and possibly others in the northern part of the province – sometimes ate the berries of a related species, Red Bearberry. The Ktunaxa name for cultivated crabapples is the same as the name for Kinnikinnick berries, because they are similar in taste and texture. Kinnikinnick berries are seldom eaten today. Many people note that grouse like to eat them, especially in winter.

The use of Kinnikinnick leaves for tobacco by indigenous peoples in North America is well known. Before contact with Europeans, most of the groups in the southern interior smoked Kinnikinnick, but apparently not the Carrier or other northern Athapaskan peoples. According to Father Morice, the Carrier had no knowledge of smoking until after 1792, when they learned about it from European traders. To prepare the leaves for smoking, people toasted them beside a fire until they were crisp and brown (nowadays they are browned in an oven). They smoked Kinnikinnick alone or mixed with wild or commercial tobacco (see Appendix 3). Some people say Kinnikinnick leaves are mild, but others claim that they will make you dizzy or even unconscious if you are not accustomed to smoking them. The smoke has a sweet smell. The Nlaka'pamux also used the young leaves to make a tea by boiling them or merely immersing them in boiling water. This tea was drunk as a beverage, but also had medicinal applications, as a tonic.

Creeping Snowberry

(Heather Family)

Gaultheria hispidula
(L.) Muhl. ex Bigelow
(Ericaceae)

Botanical Description

Creeping Snowberry is a creeping evergreen shrub. Its slender stems are covered with flattened brownish hairs. Small teardrop-shaped leaves, closely spaced along the stem, are thick, leathery and dotted on the underside with brown whisker-like hairs. The flowers, which appear in June and early July, grow at the nodes; they are pinkish, bell-shaped and nodding. The fruits are white, hairy berries that ripen in late July and August; edible in small amounts, the berries are juicy and have a mild wintergreen fragrance and taste. *Gaultheria hispidula* is also known as *Chiogenes hispidula*.

Habitat: commonly found in Black Spruce bogs or similar habitats growing on mossy hummocks or rotting logs.

Distribution in British Columbia: low to medium elevations in the central interior.

Aboriginal Use

Secwepemc people eat the small, sweet berries. Mary Thomas, a Secwepemc elder, knows Creeping Snowberries well. She recalls her mother once gathering big bags full of them from boggy meadows near the present site of Salmon Arm. People picked the berries in summer, and dried and stored them for winter use. They also made a fragrant tea from the berries and leaves; and pregnant women bathed in the tea-like solution.

Warning

Oil of Wintergreen is closely related to aspirin (acetylsalicylic acid) – anyone who is allergic to aspirin should not use wintergreen or its relatives. Children should not eat large quantities of Creeping Snowberries.

Labrador Tea
Trapper's Tea
(Heather Family)

Ledum groenlandicum Oeder
L. glandulosum Nutt.
(Ericaceae)

Other Names: "Swamp Tea", "Hudson's Bay Tea", "Muskeg Tea", "Indian Tea".

Botanical Description

Labrador Tea and Trapper's Tea are scraggly shrubs, 50 to 200 cm high, forming dense patches. The leaves, crowded toward the tops of the twigs, are oblong with inrolled margins. The young leaves are light green and point upward; older leaves are dark green to reddish and point groundward. Young Labrador Tea leaves have dense white fuzz on the undersides, which becomes rust-coloured with age. Trapper's Tea leaves are smooth beneath. The flowers are white, in dense terminal clusters, and the seed capsules are brown and woody. *Ledum groenlandicum* is also called *L. palustre* ssp. *groenlandicum.*

Habitat: peat bogs, muskegs and moist coniferous forests in acidic soils, usually in association with sphagnum moss.

Labrador Tea (left) and Trapper's Tea (below).

Distribution in British Columbia: *Ledum groenlandicum* is common throughout the province. *L. glandulosum* is widespread and locally common at mid elevations in the southern two-thirds of the province, but not on the coast.

Aboriginal Use

As the common names of these shrubs indicate, the leaves were a common source of tea, not only in British Columbia, but across North America. Aboriginal people picked the leaves from August to April, depending on the traditions of the group using them. Some, such as the Okanagan, picked the entire branch tips, twigs and all, whereas others used only the leaves. According to J.J. Honigmann (1946), the Denethah used the flowers as well as – or instead of – the leaves. Various recipes were used in different parts of the province. A handful of fresh or dried leaves simmered in a litre of water for 15 minutes or more yields a pleasant drink, although some people like it stronger. It has a pleasant aroma and taste and is good with or without sugar. The leaves can also add a pleasant flavour to regular or mint teas.

Labrador Tea and Trapper's Tea have many medicinal attributes as well. Some Secwepemc people believe that drinking a large quantity of either tea will counteract the effects of Poison Ivy. The teas were also used as a heart medicine or for indigestion, and were given to a mother after childbirth to ease the pain and relax her. The Stl'atl'imx drank these teas to relieve diarrhoea. Some people gave them to their dogs in a lukewarm drink as a tonic.

There is some question about whether British Columbia First Peoples began using the leaves of these plants as tea before or after the coming of Europeans. The name "Hudson's Bay Tea", used by many aboriginal peoples, suggests the latter. Many of the local aboriginal names also imply a recent beginning to the use of this tea. For example, the Ktunaxa name is derived from "McKay's Tea", presumably after a local Hudson's Bay factor. Another Ktunaxa name translates simply as "peoples' tea".

Warning

Two similar shrubs, Swamp Laurel (*Kalmia polifolia*) and Bog Rosemary (*Andromeda polifolia*), contain poisonous compounds and are known to be toxic to livestock. They are similar in growth form and habitat to Labrador Tea and Trapper's Tea, but can be distinguished by their shinier leaves and pink flowers. The two *Ledum* species also contain these compounds, but apparently in lower concentrations, because both have been used in tea for a long time. Also, some people who have tried Labrador Tea or Trapper's Tea report that they have diuretic properties and that they cause drowsiness. Others have experienced no such reactions, but it is probably best to drink only a weak solution in a moderate amount. As with almost every type of food, excessive use could be harmful.

Dwarf Blueberry *Vaccinium caespitosum* Michx.
(Heather Family) (Ericaceae)

Other Names: Mountain Blueberry, Dwarf Mountain Blueberry, Low-bush Blueberry.

Botanical Description
Dwarf Blueberry is a low, tufted shrub up to 30 cm high with yellowish-green to reddish branches. The leaves are bluish-green, small and oval, tapering at the base, with the

widest part above the middle. The leaf tips are bluntly pointed and finely toothed. The small, whitish to pink, urn-shaped flowers are borne singly in the leaf axils. The berries are globular, 6 to 8 mm in diameter and light blue to blackish blue with a pale waxy coating; they are sweet tasting.

Habitat: wet meadows to moist rocky ridges, usually at higher elevations; common above the timberline.

Distribution in British Columbia: common throughout the province.

Aboriginal Use
Dwarf Blueberries, though small and low-growing, are extremely popular among all interior First Peoples; many consider them the sweetest, best-flavoured kind of blueberries. Dwarf Blueberries ripen in August

or September, depending on the elevation and latitude. People usually harvested them with a comb made of wood or salmon backbone, because they grow too close to the ground to be picked like other berries. Some people collected them by lying on the ground, putting one hand under the branches and the other on top, then wriggling the fingers until the berries dropped off into the lower hand. Dwarf Blueberries have to be thoroughly cleaned and sorted, because they can have many leaves and twigs mixed in with them. People ate them fresh, as a treat, or mashed and dried in cakes. Some people freeze or can them nowadays, but many no longer use them because they are so difficult to pick. Many people have favourite local picking spots; Dwarf Blueberries are often more plentiful a few years after a fire. They were a common trading item in the early days.

Mountain Bilberry

Vaccinium membranaceum Dougl. ex Hook.

(Heather Family) (Ericaceae)

Other Names: Black Mountain Huckleberry, Black Huckleberry, Twin-leaved Huckleberry.

Botanical Description
Mountain Bilberry is a branching deciduous shrub, often low, but capable of growing up to 2 metres tall. It has yellow-green twigs and greyish shredded bark on the older branches. The leaves are elliptical and pointed, with finely serrated edges; they often turn bright red-orange in autumn. The flowers are single and creamy-pink. The berries are large, spherical, dark purple or black, and sweet; because they have no waxy coating, they are conspicuously shiny.

Habitat: mountain slopes and clearings, and open coniferous woods.

Distribution in British Columbia: throughout the province, but rare on northern Vancouver Island and in the north; not found on Haida Gwaii and the west coast of Vancouver Island.

Aboriginal Use

All interior aboriginal peoples ate Mountain Bilberries when available. They harvested the large dark berries from July to September, depending on the elevation; as the season progressed, the women would venture higher into the mountains to get them. People ate the berries fresh, or they dried them in the sun or, if the weather was bad, over a small fire. Today, they freeze or can them, or make jam with them. The Okanagan once sold large quantities of Mountain Bilberries to European settlers. In a narrative of the Lakes people, Mountain Bilberry was first introduced to the Kettle Falls area as a gift from the Mountain Goat brothers. It was named "sweet berry" by Eagle, who married the eldest brother in appreciation of the gift.

Birds and other animals are also fond of these berries. Berries of a similar species, *Vaccinium globulare*, though rare in British Columbia, were a major food of the Ktunaxa and Flathead people of Montana.

Canada Blueberry   *Vaccinium myrtilloides* Michx.
(Heather Family)   (Ericaceae)

Other Names: Velvet-leaf Blueberry, Sour-top Blueberry.

Botanical Description

Canada Blueberry is a low deciduous shrub that grows up to 40 cm high in dense patches. The leaves are oval to elliptical, thin, smooth-edged and velvety. The small flowers are greenish white tinged with pink, and

grow in short terminal clusters, expanding when the leaves are half grown. The medium-sized berries grow in clusters; they are blue, with a whitish waxy film, and sweet. A synonym for *Vaccinium myrtilloides* is *V. canadense.*

Habitat: shaded woods, dry muskeg and wooded rocky outcrops.

Distribution in British Columbia: mainly confined to the Kootenays and the central interior as a native plant, but also common in the lower Fraser River valley and the Delta area, where it was apparently introduced as a commercial crop plant.

Aboriginal Use
The Ktunaxa, Carrier and Sekani ate Canada Blueberries, and so did other groups within their range. They ate the berries fresh or dried them in cakes for winter, as they did other types of blueberries.

Low Bilberry   *Vaccinium myrtillus* L.
(Heather Family)   (Ericaceae)

Other Names: Dwarf Bilberry, Whortleberry.

Botanical Description
Low Bilberry is a low bushy shrub 20 to 30 cm high, with ridged greenish branches. The leaves are small, 10 to 30 mm long, oval to elliptical, sharply toothed and prominently veined on the undersides. The flowers, borne singly in the leaf axils, are small, pinkish and urn-shaped. The fruits are spherical, 5 to 8 mm in diameter, varying from dark red to blue-black, without a waxy coating. They are juicy and sweetish. *Vaccinium myrtillus* is also known as *V. oreophilum.*

Habitat: moist open woods at high altitudes.

Distribution in British Columbia: confined to the southeastern corner in the Kootenays.

Aboriginal Use
The Ktunaxa, Secwepemc and Carrier gathered Low Bilberries from August to early autumn and ate them fresh or dried. Low Bilberries

were popular and are still used today. To dry them, people boiled the berries in a kettle, kneaded the pulp, and spread it over a small rack. Nowadays, people make jam with Low Bilberries.

Oval-leaved Blueberry (Heather Family)

Vaccinium ovalifolium Sm. (Ericaceae)

Other Names: Oval-leaved Bilberry, Mountain Blueberry, High-bush Blueberry.

Botanical Description

Oval-leaved Blueberry is a slender deciduous shrub that grows up to 150 cm tall. It has yellowish twigs and greyish older branches. The leaves are thin, oval and rounded at the ends, with generally smooth edges. The flowers, appearing before the leaves mature, are solitary and pinkish. The berries are of good size and flavour; they are dark blue, but usually covered with a thick, waxy coating that gives them a greyish appearance.

Habitat: moist coniferous forests, along shaded stream banks, and in dry, open woods.

Distribution in British Columbia: confined to southern and central British Columbia below 56°N latitude; common on Vancouver Island, Haida Gwaii and the mainland coast, and in the southeastern interior.

Aboriginal Use

Most southern interior peoples ate Oval-leaved Blueberries, as did the Wet'suwet'en and other northern groups who had access to them. But in some areas, they were not as popular as other types of blueberries and huckleberries because of their coarser seeds and tendency to rot easily. Oval-leaved Blueberries are among the first berries to ripen, sometimes as early as the first part of July, but can be found later in the season at higher elevations. People eat them fresh or dried or in jam. They usually gather them at the same time as Mountain Bilberries. Some people like the Oval-leaved Blueberry better, while others prefer the bilberries. Sometimes, Secwepemc women cooked the berries over a small fire as they were picked, allowing them to soften so that they would take up less room and require fewer baskets when carried home. Later, they recooked and dried them; if they left the berries after the preliminary cooking, they would go mouldy. When people cooked the berries, they collected the juice in birch-bark baskets and either added it a little at a time to the berries as they dried or set it aside. When the juice cools it has the consistency of jelly and makes a delicious treat.

Bog Cranberry   *Vaccinium oxycoccus* L.
(Heather Family)   (Ericaceae)

Other Names: Wild Cranberry, Moss Cranberry.

Botanical Description
Bog Cranberry is a slender, creeping, vine-like shrub with tiny oval leaves spaced evenly along the trailing stem. The leaves are dark green with whitish undersides. The flowers, borne singly on slender, nodding stems, are deep pink with recurved petals and protruding stamens. The berries, round to somewhat elongated, remain hard and green well into autumn, usually turning red and becoming softer after the first frost. In taste, they resemble commercial cranberries.

Habitat: restricted to muskegs and peat bogs, always in association with sphagnum moss.

Distribution in British Columbia: throughout the province. This species is treated by some botanists in a separate genus, *Oxycoccus*, and is differentiated into two or three species: *O. macrocarpus*, *O. oxycoccos* and *O. quadripetalus*. These are all similar and here are treated as a single species.

Aboriginal Use

Bog Cranberries are closely related to commercial cranberries. Aboriginal peoples throughout the interior ate these tart wild berries whenever they were available. They gathered Bog Cranberries from late summer to late fall – those they harvested early were usually stored until they ripened. People ate them raw or boiled with meat; some groups, such as the Lower Stl'atl'imx and Carrier, even dried them for winter. The Nisga'a preserved Bog Cranberries by boiling them and mixing them with oil; then, in winter, they served them as a dessert, whipped up with snow and Eulachon grease. The Ktunaxa call them "fool-hen's berries" because grouse like to eat them.

Grouseberry

(Heather Family)

Vaccinium scoparium
Leiberg ex Coville
(Ericaceae)

Other Names: Red Alpine Huckleberry, Dwarf Red Whortleberry, Dwarf Red Huckleberry, Small-leaved Huckleberry.

Botanical Description
Grouseberry is a low, densely branching shrub up to 25 cm tall, with numerous erect branches that are ridged and greenish. The leaves are sparse, small (usually less than 1 cm long), oval to lance-shaped, pointed and finely toothed; they are thin and light green, and the upper surface is shiny. Small, pink urn-shaped flowers are borne singly in the leaf axils. The berries are bright red, up to 5 mm across and sweet.

Habitat: in open woods and on slopes at subalpine and alpine elevations.

Distribution in British Columbia: restricted to the southern interior, south of 52°N latitude, except in the Rocky Mountains, where it extends almost to 54°N.

Aboriginal Use
The Ktunaxa, Nlaka'pamux, Okanagan, and Secwepemc gathered the tiny red berries in late summer, at the same time as Dwarf Blueberries, and usually ate them fresh. Grouseberries are too small to be picked efficiently with the fingers, so most people harvested them in the same manner as they gathered Dwarf Blueberries, with combs of wood or bone. The Ktunaxa name for Grouseberry means "comb".

Bog Blueberry
(Heather Family)

Vaccinium uliginosum L.
(Ericaceae)

Other Names: Bog Bilberry, Bog Huckleberry, Whortleberry.

Botanical Description
Bog Blueberry is a low deciduous shrub that grows up to 50 cm high. It has many branches, often spreading. The leaves are small, rounded, bluish-green, broadest at the tip and smooth-edged. The flowers are small and pink. The berries are 6 to 8 mm in diameter, dark blue with a waxy coating, and sweet.

Habitat: muskegs and peat bogs, associated with sphagnum moss.

Distribution in British Columbia: abundant on the coast, particularly on Haida Gwaii, and in the northern interior; not generally found in the central and southern interior.

Aboriginal Use
First Peoples of the northern interior – the Tahltan, Kaska, Dene-thah and others – used Bog Blueberry extensively. The people of the Great Slave Lake area in the Northwest Territories gathered the berries in large quantities during a two-week period toward the end of August;

they ate them raw or boiled them in grease and stored them for winter. The Dene-thah apparently did not store them, but only ate them fresh. The Lower Stl'atl'imx also ate Bog Blueberries, but most other southern interior groups did not have access to them.

Low-bush Cranberry

(Heather Family)

Vaccinium vitis-idaea L. ssp. *minus* (Lodd.) Hult.

(Ericaceae)

Other Names: Mountain Cranberry, Rock Cranberry, Lingon Berry.

Botanical Description
A low evergreen mat-forming shrub, Low-bush Cranberry grows up to 30 cm tall. The branches are tufted and the leaves are small, leathery,

shiny and oblong with rounded tips. The pinkish flowers are borne in short terminal clusters. The berries are bright red, up to a centimetre in diameter (but usually smaller), soft when ripe, and acidic.

Habitat: muskegs, peat bogs, rocky barrens and coniferous woods.

Distribution in British Columbia: common in the north; sporadic on the southern coast and in the southern Rocky Mountains.

Aboriginal Use
The Nisga'a, Wet'suwet'en, Sekani, Tahltan, Dene-thah and other Athapaskan peoples ate Low-bush Cranberries. Like Bog Cranberries, Low-bush Cranberries are tart tasting and hard until they are exposed to frost. The Nisga'a gathered them in fall, along with Bog Cranberries, boiled them, and mixed them with oil for storage. In winter, people mixed Low-bush Cranberries with snow, whipped them into a froth with Eulachon grease, and served this as a dessert.

Waxy Currant
(Gooseberry Family)

Ribes cereum Dougl.
(Grossulariaceae)

Other Name: Desert Currant.

Botanical Description
Waxy Currant is a many-branched shrub that grows 10 to 150 cm tall. The branches are greyish-brown. The leaves are small, bluish-grey, rounded, and shallowly 3- or 5-lobed or merely toothed. The flowers are inconspicuous, whitish, tubular and sticky; they are borne in clusters of two to eight. The berries are oval, 6 to 8 mm long, red to orange, translucent, dry, seedy and somewhat insipid.

Habitat: dry rocky slopes, often with sagebrush and cactus.

Distribution in British Columbia: restricted to the dry southern interior, especially in the Similkameen River valley and Okanagan Valley, extending as far north as the Kamloops area.

Aboriginal Use
Though rather tasteless and dry, Waxy Currants were eaten by the Nlaka'pamux, Okanagan, Stl'atl'imx and southern Secwepemc. They ripen in June or July. People picked them casually and ate them fresh, rather than drying them for winter storage. The Okanagan compare their taste to that of dry, cultivated crabapples. Many aboriginal people thought Waxy Currants were a good health food – the Nlaka'pamux and Secwepemc ate them to relieve diarrhoea and to gain strength. The Okanagan noted that grouse like to eat the berries. In Upper Nlaka'pamux country, Waxy Currant is said to be the earliest shrub to sprout leaves.

Northern Black Currant

(Gooseberry Family)

Ribes hudsonianum
Richards.
(Grossulariaceae)

Other Names: Wild Black Currant, Hudson Bay Currant.

Botanical Description

Northern Black Currant is an upright shrub that grows 50 to 150 cm tall. It is covered with small, yellow crystalline glands that exude a distinctive sweetish odour. The leaves, usually 4 to 10 cm wide, are maple-leaf shaped, with three to five broadly pointed lobes. Numerous small,

whitish flowers grow in long, erect clusters. The fruits are 7 to 12 mm long, black and usually covered with a whitish waxy coating; they are somewhat bitter, and unpalatable to some people.

Habitat: along shaded streams, moist woods, and thickets at the edge of mountain meadows.

Distribution in British Columbia: throughout the province east of the Coast and Cascade mountains.

Aboriginal Use

The Nlaka'pamux, Okanagan, Stl'atl'imx, southern Secwepemc, Carrier, Wet'suwet'en, Sekani and Dene-thah ate Northern Black Currants. Some liked them, but others ate them only as a last resort. According to some Nlaka'pamux elders, the presence of currant bushes around the edge of a lake is a sure indication that it contains fish; in some traditional stories, the currants that drop into the water are transformed into trout. The Carrier called this fruit "toad berry" and did not eat it very much. Neither they nor the Secwepemc use it now. The Nlaka'pamux and Okanagan note that bears love to eat it.

Interior First Peoples also ate other types of currants in limited quantities. The Wet'suwet'en and possibly others ate Red Currants. The Nlaka'pamux and Stl'atl'imx used Red-flowering Currants, the latter usually mixing them with Northern Black Currants or other fruit. The Lower Nlaka'pamux ate Stink Currants. They, the Okanagan and the

Ktunaxa ate Sticky Currants, though infrequently. The Flathead Salish of Montana ate the fruits of the Golden Currant. But no group used any of the currants much; they seldom dried or stored them for winter.

Wild Gooseberries:

Wild Gooseberry	*Ribes divaricatum* **Dougl.**
Black Gooseberry	*R. inerme* **Rydb.**
Mountain Gooseberry	*R. irriguum* **Dougl.**
Smooth Gooseberry	*R. oxyacanthoides* **L.**
(Gooseberry Family)	**(Grossulariaceae)**

Other Names: Coastal Black Gooseberry (*R. divaricatum*); White-stemmed Gooseberry (*R. inerme*); Idaho Gooseberry, Inland Black Gooseberry (*R. irriguum*); Northern Gooseberry (*R. oxyacanthoides*).

Botanical Description

Wild gooseberries are erect to spreading deciduous shrubs, usually 1 to 2 metres tall, armed with bristles and stout thorns at the leaf nodes. The leaves are small and maple-leaf shaped, with three to five deep, toothed lobes. The flowers are small and greenish to purplish, with recurving petal-like sepals; they grow in drooping  clusters of two to four. The fruits are round and smooth, reddish purple to deep bluish-purple or purplish-black, and of good flavour when ripe. These species closely resemble one another. They can be distinguished as follows: Wild Gooseberry and Black Gooseberry have stamens at least twice as long as the petals, while Mountain Gooseberry stamens are about equal to the petals in length. The sepals of Wild Gooseberry are purplish, while those of Black Gooseberry and Mountain Gooseberry are greenish. Smooth Gooseberry differs from the other three species in having smaller flowers and numerous (usually) internodal spines along the stems (see Swamp Gooseberry on page 129), whereas the others are mainly armed with a few nodal spines or thorns.

Habitat: Wild Gooseberry grows in open woods, prairies and moist hillsides; Black Gooseberry is found along stream banks, in thickets at the edge of meadows and on open to wooded mountain ridges; Mountain Gooseberry grows in moist to dry canyons and open to wooded hillsides; and Smooth Gooseberry grows along streams, and on prairies and lower mountains.

Distribution in British Columbia: Wild Gooseberry is generally restricted to west of the coast and Cascade Mountains, Black Gooseberry to the east slopes of the Cascades, and Mountain Gooseberry and Smooth Gooseberry are widespread in the interior east of the Coast and Cascade mountains, extending into the far north.

Aboriginal Use

All wild gooseberries were eaten within their respective areas of distribution. But most aboriginal people did not use large quantities of them and seldom gathered enough to store for the winter. But the Lakes people picked enough to dry them in cakes, alone or mixed with other berries (especially Saskatoons), and store them for later use. Today, people in some areas still eat wild gooseberries; if enough can be gathered, they make excellent jellies and pies, alone or mixed with other types of berries. Wild gooseberries have to be picked just as they are turning black; when green they are too sour, and after ripening they soon fall off the branches. Sometimes, people picked the green berries and allowed them to ripen. The Okanagan formerly mixed mashed wild gooseberries with Bitter-root and traded them to the Nlaka'pamux people for dried salmon.

Swamp Gooseberry
(Gooseberry Family)

Ribes lacustre (Pers.) Poir.
(Grossulariaceae)

Other Names: Swamp Currant, Prickly Currant.

Botanical Description

Swamp Gooseberry is an erect to spreading deciduous shrub, mostly 1 to 1.5 metres high, with light reddish-brown stems. The stems are usually thickly covered with thin sharp spines, and have thicker thorns at the nodes. The leaves are small and shaped like maple leaves, with sharp deeply indented lobes. The flowers are small and inconspicuous, usually reddish, in drooping clusters of 7 to 15. The berries, also clustered, are small, dark purple to blackish, shiny and covered with bristles.

Habitat: moist, open woods and stream banks, often on rotten stumps and damp rocky cliffs, from sea level to subalpine forest.

Distribution in British Columbia: throughout the province, common in coniferous and mixed woods.

Aboriginal Use

The Stl'atl'imx, Nlaka'pamux, Okanagan, Ktunaxa, Sekani and probably other interior groups ate Swamp Gooseberries fresh or cooked, despite their small size. Nowadays, people often make jam with them. The Lower Stl'atl'imx also boiled the berries to make a tea, which they said was especially good for colds. The Nlaka'pamux call Swamp Gooseberries "hairy-face", because they are covered with stiff black bristles.

The Okanagan made a refreshing menthol-flavoured tea from the leaves, branches and inner bark of this shrub. Called "catnip tea" by some people, it was made by singeing off the spines and boiling the fresh or dried branches for a few minutes or simply by steeping them in boiling water. The resulting beverage was drunk not only as a tea but as a medicine for colds and diarrhoea.

Ball-head Waterleaf

(Waterleaf Family)

Hydrophyllum capitatum Dougl. ex Benth.
(Hydrophyllaceae)

Botanical Description

Ball-head Waterleaf is a low-growing herb, 10 to 40 cm high, with solitary or clustered stems. It has a short, deep-seated rhizome from which

a cluster of thick, fibrous roots descends. Its few leaves are long-stemmed and relatively large, deeply cleft into seven to eleven leaflets, or bluntly pointed and frequently lobed. The flowers are small, usually lavender or purplish blue, with prominent stamens; they are tightly clustered in round heads, 3 cm or more in diameter.

Habitat: woodlands, moist open slopes and meadows, from lowlands to well up in the mountains.

Distribution in British Columbia: in the south, east of the Cascade Mountains; common in Botanie Valley.

Aboriginal Use

The Nlaka'pamux, southern Secwepemc and Okanagan dug up the long, fleshy roots of Ball-head Waterleaf in late spring. They always cooked them by boiling or steaming, and often ate them with other types of roots, such as Yellow Avalanche Lily bulbs. Ball-head Waterleaf is common at Botanie Valley, but is no longer used. Cattle and other livestock like to eat the leaves and roots.

Bugleweed
(Mint Family)

Lycopus uniflorus Michx.
(Lamiaceae or Labiatae)

Other Name: Water Horehound.

Botanical Description
Bugleweed is a slender herb, 10 to 40 cm tall, with simple or occasionally branched, upright stems arising from a small, thick tuber; it often reproduces vegetatively by runners. The stems are square. The leaves are opposite, lance-shaped and pointed, with coarsely toothed margins. The flowers are small and white, growing in dense clusters at the leaf nodes.

Habitat: stream banks, marshes and peat bogs, from lowlands to upper elevations.

Distribution in British Columbia: along the entire coast near sea level, and in the middle and southern interior at higher elevations.

Aboriginal Use
Few would suspect that this inconspicuous member of the mint family was used as a vegetable. But the Nlaka'pamux, Secwepemc, Okanagan and possibly the Ktunaxa ate the fleshy tubers of Bugleweed after steaming them in pits. The tubers are said to have a sweet, pleasant taste, reminiscent of a mild radish. Today, aboriginal people scarcely remember using Bugleweed – few even recognize the plant or its aboriginal names.

Fireweed
(Evening Primrose Family)

Epilobium angustifolium L.
(Onagraceae)

Other Names: Willow Herb, Blooming Sally.

Botanical Description
Fireweed is a tall smooth-stemmed herbaceous perennial, with spreading roots and alternate, smooth-edged, lance-shaped leaves resembling those of narrow-leaved willows. The flowers are red-purple with four petals; they grow in long terminal clusters and are very showy. They bloom throughout the summer in sequence from bottom to top. The seed capsules are long and narrow, splitting longitudinally on all four sides to reveal rows of small, parachuted seeds. The seeds travel on the wind for long distances.

Habitat: open clearings, logged areas, burns and along roadsides, in extensive patches. In summer, blooming Fireweed often colours entire hillsides purple.

Distribution in British Columbia: widespread throughout the province.

Fireweed on a hillside (left) and picked shoots (below).

Aboriginal Use

The inner part of the stem, especially in young plants, is sweet and succulent. Most interior peoples ate Fireweed stalks: the Nlaka'pamux, Stl'atl'imx, Secwepemc, Carrier, Wet'suwet'en, Sekani, Nisga'a and probably others; but not the Okanagan and Ktunaxa, according to available information. People sought out Fireweed plants in the springtime before they bloomed. They broke off the stems, stripped off the leaves, split open the outer part longitudinally with the fingernail, and ate the pith raw. Sometimes, they boiled or steamed the stems, but this was less common. Some interior peoples use the leafy stems of Fireweed as flavouring or matting in root-cooking pits or earth ovens.

Within the last century, some Japanese-Canadians and others of Asian heritage have adopted it as a green vegetable. Fireweed leaves are used as a tea in some parts of Russia. Animals, both wild and domestic, like to eat Fireweed.

Spring Beauty
(Purslane Family)

Claytonia lanceolata Pursh
(Portulacaceae)

Other Name: "Indian Potato", "Mountain Potato".

Botanical Description

Spring Beauty is a herbaceous perennial, 5 to 15 cm tall, with one to several stems arising from a shallow spherical corm, which may be 5 cm or more in diameter. The corm is brown-skinned and white inside.

Spring Beauty growing with Yellow Avalanche Lilies. (See also page 25.)

Basal leaves are seldom present at flowering time. Each stem bears, near its midpoint, two opposite, lance-shaped to oval, pointed leaves that are commonly 5 to 20 mm broad and 15 to 60 mm long. The flowers are usually white, sometimes with pink lines, or occasionally deep pink, with five petals and two broad sepals; about a centimetre or more wide, the flowers grow in elongated terminal clusters of 3 to 20. The seeds are small, black and shiny.

Habitat: dry sagebrush foothills to damp alpine meadows, often abundant near snowdrifts. In some localities Spring Beauty is so plentiful it colours entire meadows white.

Distribution in British Columbia: usually at higher elevations in the central and southern part of the province on both sides of the Cascade Mountains, but most abundant in interior mountain meadows.

Aboriginal Use

As the name "Indian Potato" suggests, Spring Beauty was an important source of carbohydrates for aboriginal peoples of the interior. The Nlaka'pamux, Stl'atl'imx, Okanagan, Secwepemc, Ktunaxa, Carrier and Tsilhqot'in, and possibly the Sekani, ate the small, spherical corms in large quantities. They usually dug up the corms just after the plants flowered, from late May to late June, depending on the elevation. If harvested earlier, they are too watery. In Okanagan territory they are ready to dig just after the Bitter-root harvest. The size of the corm can usually be determined by the number of stems it bears: a corm with two or three stems may be 3 cm wide, one having ten stems might be 5 cm

across and one with fifteen stems could be as big as 8 cm in diameter, but such large corms are seldom encountered.

Spring Beauty corms are not deep, usually 3 to 8 cm below the surface. In the past, people used a short digging stick to pry out the corms. Nowadays, some people use a small shovel. The best way to dig them up is to turn over sections of turf with a shovel, select the largest corms and replant the smaller ones to allow them to continue growing.

If people gathered only a small crop, they cooked the corms and ate them immediately. First, they washed the corms, then steamed them in underground pits or boiled them like potatoes with very little water. The Stl'atl'imx used to wrap them in cloth and steam them like plum pudding. Spring Beauty corms resemble potatoes in taste, but are sweeter. Sometimes they were cooked with other roots, such as Yellowbell bulbs. They might be flavoured with "Indian Celery".

If people dug up many corms, they could store them for later use. The Secwepemc, Carrier and Tsilhqot'in often strung them on a line of sinew, buckskin, or Indian Hemp or other plant fibre, and hung them up near a chimney or fire-hole to smoke them. After several weeks, the corms could be stored and eaten without further preparation. People also dried Spring Beauty corms by spreading them on mats, or they cooked and mashed them, then formed them into loaves or cakes, which they dehydrated slowly. But many Okanagan and some Secwepemc people did not dry them; instead they stored them like potatoes in earth pits about 60 cm deep, lined and covered with pine needles and cottonwood bark. Thus insulated, the corms would not freeze in winter and could easily be dug out from under the snow.

"Indian Potatoes" could also be harvested in the fall, and are said to be sweetest at this time. Voles, pikas, marmots and other small mammals also dig them up and hide them in caches as a winter food supply. An easy and common way of getting a meal was to locate one of these caches. People were careful not to take all of the cached food, or they left a gift for the animal that collected it.

Note
Spring Beauty is rare in some areas. Traditional harvesting methods effectively sustained its populations. But today, livestock have reduced its productivity by grazing and trampling. If you wish to sample the corms, be careful not to harvest too many, and always leave the smaller corms behind for repropogation.

Bitter-root

Lewisia rediviva Pursh, L. columbiana (Howell ex Gray) Robins. and L. pygmaea (Gray) Robins.

(Purslane Family) (Portulacaceae)

Other Names: Sand Rose, Desert Rose, Rock Rose, Spatlum, Spitlum.

Botanical Description

Bitter-root is a low stemless perennial arising from a branching deep-seated fleshy taproot, which is grey-skinned with a white inner core that may turn pink on exposure to the air. The leaves, clustered at the surface of the ground, are small, narrow and fleshy; they usually begin to wither by the time the flowers open. *Lewisa rediviva* flowers are borne singly on short, leafless stems, sometimes five or six per plant; they are 4 cm or more wide, with up to 18 elongated petals and numerous stamens. The flowers vary from white to deep pink, and are strikingly beautiful; they close at night and reopen with the morning sun. *L.*

columbiana has small white to rose-coloured flowers with fewer petals than *L. rediviva*; the flowers grow in loose clusters on stems 10 to 30 cm long. *L. pygmaea* has fewer, larger flowers (up to 2 cm wide), with about seven white to pale lavender petals; the flowers grow alone on short stems. All three species have round, dark brown, shiny seeds, 6 to 20 per flower.

Habitat: *L. rediviva* grows in dry, gravely or sandy soil from sagebrush plains to lower mountains, *L. columbiana* is found on exposed gravel banks and rocky slopes at higher elevations; and *L. pygmaea* grows on open moist to dry, gravely slopes in the mountains to above the timberline.

Distribution in British Columbia: *L. rediviva* is restricted to the driest parts of the southern interior, especially in the Thompson River and Okanagan valleys and also in the southern Kootenay River valley near the Montana border; *L. columbiana* occurs in southern British Columbia on both sides of the Cascade Mountains; *L. pygmaea* occurs sporadically on high mountain slopes from Vancouver Island to the Rocky Mountains and is considered rare.

Aboriginal Use

To many Okanagan, Ktunaxa and Upper Nlaka'pamux people, Bitter-root was the most important of all edible roots. The Lower Nlaka'pamux, Stl'atl'imx and Secwepemc were also fond of it and used it whenever it was available. Even today it is a popular vegetable, but unless it grows nearby, it is extremely difficult to obtain, even from friends or relatives.

The best time to dig Bitter-roots is just before the plants flower, when the buds are still tightly closed but showing a pink hue. This varies from early to late May, depending on the elevation. Different populations of Bitter-root vary considerably in the size and bitterness of their roots. Plants of higher elevations (over 750 metres) are said to produce larger, less bitter roots than those of the dry desert lowlands and valleys. People pry up the roots with a digging stick; made of wood or (more recently) iron, the stick has a sharp, often curved point at one end and a cross-piece for a handle. After cleaning a root of leaves and buds, the gatherer rolls it between the hands or on a rock to loosen its skin, then pulls the skin off in one piece. Inside the root, near the top, is a small red-orange structure called the heart, the embryo of next year's growth. This is said to be, along with the skin, the bitterest part of the root – if not removed, it can make the entire root too bitter to eat. The gatherer usually removes the heart immediately by splitting open the top of the root and pulling it out with the fingers.

The peeled, de-hearted roots can be eaten fresh after baking or boiling a short time, or strung on strings or sticks or spread out on mats to

Dried Bitter-roots (left) and the heart of a Bitter-root (right). See also the dried Bitter-roots with Biscuitroots and Camas bulbs, on page 82.

dry for several days. After this they will keep all year, although some say they become more bitter the longer they are kept. Properly dried roots are almost pure white. If they are not dried right away, they turn a deep pink, but will become white again if soaked in water. Interior people used to store Bitter-roots in fibre bags, and sometimes buried the bags in earth pits lined with pine needles. Do not eat a large quantity of dried Bitter-roots – they will swell up in the stomach.

In the past, aboriginal people boiled or steamed Bitter-roots in small earth pits and almost always mixed them with other foods, especially with Saskatoon Berries. The following recipe for Bitter-root pudding, from the Pacific Region Medical Service's *Indian Foods* (1971), represents a modern adaptation of a traditional interior First Peoples' dish. Mrs Guiterrez of Douglas Lake (Secwepemc) supplied this recipe.

Combine dried Bitter-root with dried Saskatoon Berries and boil until soft, in the following proportions:

2 cups dried Bitter-root
½ cup dried Saskatoon Berries
1 cup water

Prepare a small amount of a stiff flour-and-water dough. Roll a teaspoon of this mixture between the palms of both hands to form a small noodle-like shape. Drop enough doughy noodles into the cooking berry/root mixture to give it a pudding-like consistency.

Bitter-roots can also be baked in fruit cakes. When properly prepared they are mild and pleasant tasting, though still slightly bitter to the European palate. In the past, Bitter-root was a major item of commerce in the southern interior. Its use far exceeded its natural distribution. The Okanagan traded it to the Nlaka'pamux, the Upper Nlaka'pamux to the Stl'atl'imx and Lower Nlaka'pamux, the southern Secwepemc to the northern Secwepemc, and the southern Ktunaxa to the northern Ktunaxa. Even today, people travel for many miles to get Bitter-roots, and a gift of them is highly valued.

According to Okanagan tradition, Bitter-root is the chief of all the roots. The Okanagan people used to hold a special ceremony every spring to celebrate the harvest of the first Bitter-roots, along with the first Saskatoon Berries and the first fish and game.

On occasion, the Nlaka'pamux and possibly other interior groups ate the two other species of *Lewisia* – *pygmaea* and *columbiana*. The Blackfoot of Alberta also ate *L. pygmaea*. But some Nlaka'pamux people believed that eating *L. pygmaea* would cause instant insanity. Neither species was as well liked as the real Bitter-root.

Note

Bitter-root is becoming increasingly rare due to overgrazing and human encroachment on its habitat. Do not increase the destruction of this beautiful and delicate flower by the wholesale digging of its roots. As with Spring Beauty, Bitter-root can be plentiful in certain localities, and sampling a few in such places would be harmless enough, but in places where it is scarce, it should be left alone.

Saskatoon Berry

(Rose Family)

Amelanchier alnifolia Nutt. ex Roemer

(Rosaceae)

Other Names: Service Berry, June Berry, Shad-bush.

Botanical Description

Saskatoon Berry is a highly variable deciduous shrub, 1 to 7 metres high, with smooth reddish to grey bark. It has numerous round to oval leaves that are bluish green and usually sharply toothed around the top half. The flowers, which bloom in April and May, are white and showy, with five elongated petals. They are crowded in drooping to erect clusters. Especially in the interior, the flowers often cover the bushes, creating a spectacular sight in areas where the plants are numerous. The berries, when ripe, are reddish-purple to dark blue, and sometime quite seedy. Their size, texture and taste vary considerably from plant to plant. Botanists distinguish three varieties in the Interior Salish area – var. *alnifolia*, var. *semiintegrifolia* and var. *cusickii* – but Salish peoples designate up to nine types. Further taxonomic research on this highly complex species may

reveal that indigenous peoples are more accurate in their differentiation than botanists have been.

Habitat: dry woods and open hillsides in well-drained soil.

Distribution in British Columbia: common and widespread, but most prolific in the dry woods and open slopes of the southern interior.

Aboriginal Use

Of all the berries and fruits eaten by the interior First Peoples of British Columbia, Saskatoon Berries were the most extensively used, especially in the southern and central interior. Among the northern groups, such as the Dunne-za, Sekani and Dene-thah, Saskatoons were one of the few types of vegetable foods available in quantity. So important were Saskatoon Berries that Interior Salish groups developed a classification for different varieties that is more detailed and complex than that of professional taxonomists. On the basis of habitat, blooming and ripening time, growth form, and size, colour, seediness and taste of the berries, they distinguish many varieties, each with its own particular advantages and disadvantages as a food.

The Upper Stl'atl'imx, for example, recognize six varieties: a low-bush type with small, dark, juicy berries and small seeds, ideal for drying in cakes or canning; a high-bush variety with large good-tasting berries, known as the "real Saskatoon"; another high-bush type with reddish berries that dry on the branches like raisins – a favourite of children; a rare variety with exceedingly sweet berries; one with large attractive berries that have large seeds and a bad taste, known as "rotten Saskatoon"; and a late-ripening type with small tart berries, the "bitter Saskatoon". Of these, only the low-bush variety is said to grow in the Lower Stl'atl'imx country around Pemberton. "Real Saskatoons" are often traded into this area. The Okanagan recognize eight varieties, and the Nlaka'pamux and Secwepemc each recognize several.

Saskatoon Berries are harvested in June, July or August, depending on the variety, elevation and locality. In the Secwepemc language, the eighth moon is called "Saskatoons ripen". In some areas, such as at Penticton in Okanagan country and at Big Bar in Secwepemc territory, people held a first-fruits ceremony to celebrate the beginning of the Saskatoon picking season. At Penticton, this was combined with a first-roots and first-fish-and-game ceremonies: four young women went out to dig the first Bitter-roots, four to pick the first Saskatoons, and four young men went out fishing and hunting. The proceeds from these harvests were used to give a feast for the entire tribe. At Big Bar, where there are several good Saskatoon patches, women would come from Clinton and Alkali Lake at the direction of the local chief. On a designated day, they each went out and picked only a few for themselves and their friends to eat fresh. After that they picked all they could and dried them for winter.

Interior peoples used a variety of methods to dry Saskatoon Berries, depending on the type of berry and the local custom. In general, they spread the berries on mats and dried them individually, like raisins; or they mashed and boiled them in baskets with hot rocks, then spread the mash on grass, mats or rocks to dry in cakes. Sometimes they placed the berries on racks over a fire or dried them in the sun, although most people thought it better to dry Saskatoons slowly in the shade. Often the juice was collected separately and added to the drying berry cakes a little at a time, or saved and used to marinate other foods, such as Black Tree Lichen, Bitter-roots or even dried salmon. People used the dried cakes in numerous ways. They fed chunks to their children as a snack. They soaked and boiled the cakes with Bitter-root or salmon eggs, cooked them with Tiger Lily bulbs, deer meat or bear grease, mashed them with other berries, such as Red Osier Dogwood, or they simply rehydrated them and ate them alone as a dessert. They used whole Saskatoon Berries in soups and stews, and as sweeteners in such dishes as Soapberry whip. Okanagan mothers often fed their babies Saskatoon Berry juice after weaning. Dried Saskatoons were a common trading item, especially between the interior and the coast. Saskatoons remain popular today. People eat them fresh with milk and sugar, cooked in puddings, pies and cakes, and in jams and preserves. Some produce companies are now marketing various Saskatoon Berry products, including jam and syrup.

Red Hawthorn
Black Hawthorn
(Rose Family)

Crataegus columbiana Howell
C. douglasii Lindl.
(Rosaceae)

Other Names: Red Thornberry, Black Thornberry, Red Haw, Black Haw.

Botanical Description

Hawthorns are tough, bushy deciduous shrubs or small trees. Red Hawthorn seldom exceeds 3 metres in height, whereas Black Hawthorn may reach 4 metres or more. Both shrubs are armed with sharp

Red Hawthorn.

thorns; those of Red Hawthorn are slender and 4 to 7 cm long, and those of Black Hawthorn are usually stouter and 1 to 2 cm long. The leaves are thick, roughly oval, dark green and shiny, and coarsely toothed. Red Hawthorn leaves are pointed, whereas those of Black Hawthorn are usually blunter but sharply toothed around the tip. The flowers are white and showy, in flat or rounded clusters, blooming in April and May. The berries of both species hang in clusters; they have a mealy texture, large seeds and a pleasant though somewhat bland flavour. Red Hawthorn berries are bright red and those of Black Hawthorn are shiny black.

Habitat: meadows and stream courses to dry hillsides and gullies.

Distribution in British Columbia: Red Hawthorn is found in the southern interior, from Prince George southward through the Okanagan and Kootenay valleys, and also occurs in the Peace River District; Black Hawthorn is common throughout the province south of latitude 55°N.

Aboriginal Use

Hawthorn berries ripen in August and September. The Nlaka'pamux, Okanagan, Secwepemc and Ktunaxa ate the fruits of both species; and the Stl'atl'imx, Nisga'a and Gitxsan ate those of Black Hawthorn, at least. But most people did not regard hawthorn fruits highly because of their large seeds, lack of taste, and mealy texture. Okanagan people warned their children that they would get a stomach ache if they ate too many, and the Ktunaxa considered them highly constipating. But the Stl'atl'imx, Secwepemc and Okanagan made a popular type of "bread" by

Black Hawthorn.

mashing Black Hawthorn berries, squeezing out the seeds and drying the pulp. Later, they boiled the berry-bread with deer fat and bone marrow to make a soup, or pounded and mixed it with powdered salmon bones. Today, some people make jelly from hawthorn berries, but otherwise they are little used.

Wild Strawberries:
Tall Strawberry   *Fragaria vesca* L.
Blue-leaf Strawberry   *F. virginiana* Duchesne
(Rose Family)   (Rosaceae)

Botanical Description
Wild strawberries are low-growing herbaceous perennials with conspicuous runners (stolons) for vegetative reproduction. The leaves are basal, long-stemmed and compound, with three coarsely toothed leaflets of equal size, resembling those of cultivated strawberries, but smaller. There are usually several flowers per stem; they are white, about 2 cm wide and have five petals. The berries, when ripe, are soft and pink or red, resembling miniature cultivated strawberries. Tall Strawberry has yellow-green, strongly veined leaves, tall flowering stems that often exceed the leaves in height, and elongated fruits; Blue-leaf Strawberry has smoother blue-green leaves, shorter flower stems and globular berries, which are often found right at ground-level.

Habitat: open woodlands and clearings.

Distribution in British Columbia: common and widespread in the south, but both, especially Blue-leaf Strawberry, also occur sporadically in the north.

Aboriginal Use

Wild strawberries are a favourite fruit everywhere. All interior First Peoples eat them, especially the children. In areas where both species are found, people usually recognize them as being different, but like them equally. Wild strawberries ripen from May to July, depending on elevation and latitude. People usually eat them fresh; but in the past, if they could gather large enough quantities, they dried them for later use. For drying, they were not cooked, but just mashed and spread over

grass or mats to dry in the sun. The dried berry cakes could then be cut up and eaten as a treat without further preparation, or they could be rehydrated in water and eaten alone or used as a sweetener for other foods such as Indian ice cream. A handful of dried berries would swell to fill a whole dish when soaked in water. The quality of wild strawberries can vary with weather and locality. In some years they are so sweet and plentiful that their fragrance can be detected from a long distance away.

The Nlaka'pamux and other interior peoples sometimes used strawberry flowers, leaves and stems to flavour roots in cooking-pits.

Blue-leaf Strawberry.

Common Silverweed
(Rose Family)

Potentilla anserina L.
(Rosaceae)

Other Names: Cinquefoil, "Indian Sweet Potato".

Botanical Description

Common Silverweed is a low herbaceous perennial with spreading runners and thick, fleshy roots, about 150 mm long and 5 to 10 mm thick. The leaves are basal, clumped and pinnately compound, with usually 13 to 15 oval sharply toothed leaflets that decrease in size toward the base of the leaf. The under surface is usually hairier than the upper surface. The yellow flowers, borne singly on long stalks, look like buttercup flowers.

Common Silverweed closely resembles Pacific Cinquefoil, whose roots were commonly eaten by coastal First Peoples. The main difference between them is that Common Silverweed leaves are thickly covered with whitish silky hairs, giving them a grey appearance, while the leaves of Pacific Cinquefoil are usually greener, at least on the upper surfaces.

Habitat: marshes, meadows, mud flats and pond margins, especially in alkaline soils.

Distribution in British Columbia: common in the southern interior, from the Cariboo District south, but has also been found in a few locations in the far north.

Aboriginal Use

The Nlaka'pamux, Upper Stl'atl'imx, Secwepemc and Okanagan ate the long, fleshy roots of Common Silverweed. They dug up the roots in late summer and fall, steamed or roasted them for 15 to 20 minutes, then ate them with the fingers. Silverweed roots could also be eaten raw. They have a pleasant but slightly bitter taste. Cinquefoil Lake, up the Fountain Valley in Stl'atl'imx territory, is named after this plant. The roots are not used today, and few people remember that they were once eaten.

Pin Cherry
Bitter Cherry

(Rose Family)

Prunus pensylvanica L.f.
P. emarginata
(Dougl. ex Hook.) Walpers
(Rosaceae)

Other Names: Bird Cherry, Wild Cherry; Wild Red Cherry (*P. pensylvanica*).

Botanical Description

Pin and Bitter cherries are closely related deciduous shrubs or small trees. Their bark is smooth, grey to shiny reddish purple and tends to peel off in horizontal strips. Pin Cherry seldom exceeds 5 metres in height, but Bitter Cherry may grow to 10 metres or more. The leaves are short-stemmed, 3 to 8 cm long, more or less elliptical; those of Pin Cherry are sharply pointed, tapering and finely toothed around the margins, and those of Bitter Cherry are round-tipped or bluntly

pointed and smooth-edged or finely toothed. The flowers are white, in small clusters. The fruits of Bitter Cherry are small and spherical (4 to 7 mm in diameter), and bright red, with thin, bitter flesh. Pin Cherry fruits are larger and slightly elongated (8 to 12 mm long), bright red to almost black, and usually tart but not bitter.

Habitat: moist woods and clearings, often along watercourses; particularly abundant after a fire.

Distribution in British Columbia: Pin Cherry is restricted to the central and eastern interior, generally south of 55°N latitude; Bitter Cherry is abundant across the south, especially on the coast and in the interior wet belt, from sea level to moderate elevations in the mountains.

Aboriginal Use

The Nlaka'pamux, Stl'atl'imx and Secwepemc ate sour wild cherries on a casual basis. Some of the Athapaskan groups, such as the Wet'suwet'en and probably the Carrier, also ate them. For the most part these would have been Pin Cherries, but a certain mild-flavoured variety of Bitter Cherry was also harvested. The Stl'atl'imx people, at least, were careful to note that there were two varieties of Bitter Cherry, one with fruits too bitter to eat, the other with sweet fruits. There is a large stand of Pin Cherry along the west shore of Salmon Arm on Shuswap Lake, where the Secwepemc people used to gather the cherries in mid summer. These cherries, which grow in unusually large, heavy clusters, are tart but juicy and flavourful, lacking the extreme astringency of Bitter Cherry. People usually ate wild cherries fresh, because they have large stones and are difficult to obtain in quantity.

Choke Cherry
(Rose Family)

Prunus virginiana L.
(Rosaceae)

Other Name: Wild Cherry.

Botanical Description
Choke Cherry is a shrub or small tree up to 10 metres high with pur-plish-grey bark. The leaves are el-liptical to oval, pointed and finely serrated at the margins; they are bright green above and paler be-neath. The flowers are white and numerous, in elongated terminal clusters. The ripe fruits are spher-ical, 8 to 11 mm in diameter, with  small stones and bright red to purple-black flesh, which is astringent, but sweet when ripe. Two varieties of *Prunus virginiana* are recognized: var. *demissa* and var. *melanocarpa.*

Habitat: from open woodlands to grasslands and clearings, particu-larly along watercourses.

Distribution in British Columbia: throughout the interior; particu-larly common in the south; also occurs on southeastern Vancouver Island and the adjacent mainland, but is rare and stunted.

Aboriginal Use

Despite their large stones and slight astringency, Choke Cherries were – and still are – an extremely popular food among interior First Peoples. In many areas they rank second only to Saskatoon Berries in importance as a fruit. Choke Cherries ripen in the latter half of August and throughout September, and since they grow in long clusters, can be harvested quickly and easily. Stl'atl'imx elders distinguish at least two varieties: one has translucent, red fruits that are sweet and juicy; the other has dark, purple-black fruits that, unless picked when completely ripe, are astringent, giving one the feeling of having swallowed a mouthful of cotton, hence the name "choke" cherry. But even the dark ones are pleasant tasting when fully ripe or after drying and freezing. At this stage, the astringency disappears, but the cherries are said to be constipating if too many are eaten. (See the Warning about poisonous seeds and foliage.)

Aboriginal people eat Choke Cherries fresh as a snack; they also used to dry them in large quantities for winter. They spread the cherries on mats and dried them in the sun, like raisins, or mashed and dried them in cakes. The Southern Okanagan dried them on mats for a day, then put them into a buckskin bag and pounded them into a meal, seeds and all, which they then formed into thin cakes and dried. The cakes could be soaked in water for several hours and eaten as a dessert, or pounded with salmon eggs, salmon heads and tails, or some other type of food. The Okanagan also used the dried cherries for making a tea, especially good for coughs and colds. Choke Cherries also make excellent juice, syrup and jelly, and if you have the patience to remove the stones, they are good in pies and other desserts.

Warning

Choke Cherry stones and leaves, like those of other *Prunus* species, contain toxic cyanide-producing compounds. The flesh of the fruit is not harmful, but children have been poisoned – and some have died – from eating large quantities of fresh cherries without removing the seeds. Drying the cherries with seeds intact seems to reduce or eliminate the toxicity – aboriginal people often left the seeds in the cherries when they dried them for winter. Some elders warn that eating fresh Choke Cherries with milk or ice cream will make you sick.

Wild Roses:
Prickly Rose
Dwarf Wild Rose
Common Wild Rose
Wood's Rose
(Rose Family)

Rosa acicularis Lindl.
R. gymnocarpa Nutt.
R. nutkana Presl
R. woodsii Lindl.
(Rosaceae)

Other Names: Bristly Rose (*R. acicularis*); Baldhip Rose (*R. gymnocarpa*); Nootka Rose (*R. nutkana*); Prairie Rose (*R. woodsii*).

Botanical Description
Wild roses are erect shrubs with spiny or thorny stems and compound leaves, usually with five to seven toothed leaflets, similar to those of garden roses but smaller. The flowers are pale to bright pink and have five petals, yellow centres and numerous stamens. The fruits (hips) are bright red-orange, consisting of a fleshy rind enclosing many whitish seeds. The rind is hard, but softens after the first frost; it tastes somewhat bland, but is high in Vitamin C. Prickly Rose has elongated fruits and numerous small spines on the stems and twigs. Dwarf Wild Rose has small flowers, small fruits without persisting sepals and usually densely bristled stems. Common Wild Rose has large flowers and fruits, and one or two large, flattened thorns at each node, but no small thin spines. And Wood's Rose has smaller, straight thorns; smaller, more densely clustered flowers; and relatively small, round fruits.

Habitat: Prickly Rose is found in open woods and damp meadows; Dwarf Wild Rose grows in moist shaded woods; Common Wild Rose is common along roadsides and open woods, often forming dense

Prickly Rose.

Wood's Rose.

thickets; and Wood's Rose is found in open woods and moist meadows, on prairies and creek sides.

Distribution in British Columbia: Prickly Rose occurs throughout the province east of the Coast and Cascade mountains; Dwarf Wild Rose is found on both sides of the Cascades from about 52°N latitude southward; Common Wild Rose is widespread along the coast and throughout the interior south of 56°N latitude; and Wood's Rose is common throughout the dry parts of the interior south of 56°N latitude and in the Peace River District.

Aboriginal Use

Rose hips are well known for their high Vitamin C content. Many interior aboriginal groups ate the fruits of all these roses, although usually on a casual basis or in times when other kinds of foods were scarce. In general, people ate more Prickly Rose and Common Wild Rose hips, because they are larger than those of Dwarf Wild Rose and Wood's Rose. They ate only the outside rind, discarding the prickly seeds. Rose hips ripen in late summer but often remain on the bushes after ripening, so they can be gathered frozen from the bushes in mid winter. They are said to taste better toward spring. Today some aboriginal people make rose-hip tea, jam and jelly, but these uses appear to be modern in origin. Coyotes, bears, grouse and other wild animals are said to be fond of rose hips.

The Dene-thah and Sekani made a tea from wild rose petals, and the Secwepemc, Nlaka'pamux and Okanagan made tea from the leaves, branches and inner bark of various rose species. Also, the Nlaka'pamux toasted, dried and powdered the leaves and bark of Dwarf Wild Rose and smoked the mixture, alone or with tobacco. The Okanagan and other Interior Salish placed wild rose leaves and branches in roasting pits under and over roots such as Bitter-root and "Wild Carrot" to flavour them.

Low or Dwarf Raspberries:
Dwarf Raspberry
Creeping Raspberry
Cloudberry
Trailing Wild Raspberry
(Rose Family)

Rubus pubescens Raf.
R. acaulis Michx.
R. chamaemorus L.
R. pedatus Sm.
(Rosaceae)

Botanical Description

Dwarf Raspberry is a low shrub, at first upright and later creeping, often rooting at the nodes. The leaves are long-stemmed and compound, each with three oval, pointed, sharply toothed leaflets. The flowers grow singly or in twos and threes on short side branches; their petals are elongated, usually white, or sometimes rose coloured, 10 mm or more long. The fruits resemble small raspberries, and are red and juicy. Creeping Raspberry has short erect branches. Its leaves are compound with three leaflets or simple with three lobes; when present, the leaflets are broadly oval and coarsely toothed. The flowers are pink and the fruits reddish to dark purple. Cloudberry is similar, but with simple five-lobed leaves, white flowers and yellow to salmon-coloured berries. Trailing Wild Raspberry is vine-like, and its leaves are compound with five finger-like leaflets; its flowers small and white, its fruits bright red with only two to five druplets each. *R. acaulis* is also known as *R. arcticus.*

Dwarf Raspberry.

Creeping Rasberry.

Cloudberry.

Habitat: Dwarf Raspberry grows in damp woods and bogs; Creeping Raspberry and Cloudberry are found in bogs and muskeg; and Trailing Wild Raspberry grows in damp montane forests.

Distribution in British Columbia: Dwarf Raspberry and Creeping Raspberry are found throughout the province, east of the Coast and Cascade mountains; Cloudberry occurs mainly in northern British Columbia, but is also found on the south coast, where it rarely produces fruit; and Trailing Wild Raspberry occurs throughout the province, particularly in the southern part and at higher elevations.

Aboriginal Use
Many interior First Peoples ate these berries sporadically. The Carrier, Sekani and other Athapaskan groups ate fresh Dwarf Raspberry, sometimes referring to it as Salmonberry, a name usually applied to its coastal relative, *Rubus spectabilis*, which is a tall shrub. The Secwepemc called Creeping Raspberries "false wild strawberries", and probably ate them. Cloudberry, whose range extends across northern British Columbia, was undoubtedly used by the Inland Tlingit, Tahltan, Kaska and Dene-thah, among others. And though small, Trailing Wild Raspberries were probably eaten by hunters and travellers of a number of aboriginal groups, but were of low significance as a food. The Haida and Tsimshian on the coast ate Cloudberries and Trailing Wild Raspberries.

Trailing Wild Raspberry.

Wild Raspberry
(Rose Family)

Rubus idaeus L.
(Rosaceae)

Botanical Description

Wild Raspberry is an erect prickly shrub, similar to the cultivated raspberry but usually shorter and not as robust. The bark is brownish. The leaves are usually compound with three (or sometimes five) sharply pointed leaflets, of which the terminal one is largest, as in garden raspberry leaves. The flowers are white and inconspicuous, growing in small clusters. The berries are bright red (or rarely yellow); they resemble garden raspberries but are smaller and often more flavourful.

Habitat: stream banks, open woods, clearings and talus slopes.

Distribution in British Columbia: widespread in the interior and extending to the coast along some of the northern river valleys, such as the Bella Coola and Skeena; not on Vancouver Island or Haida Gwaii.

Aboriginal Use

Wild Raspberries usually ripen in mid July. They were extremely popular everywhere. All interior First Peoples ate them fresh, or they mashed and dried them in cakes for winter storage. A favourite treat for children, described by Secwepemc elder Mary Thomas, was a fruit-leather-like preparation made from raspberries, strawberries and other juicy berries. Mary's grandmother made it by mashing fresh berries and forming them into a cake to dry, first on one side, then on the other. The centre of the cake had a smooth gelatinous consistency. Her grandmother stored the cakes in cotton flour sacks and when the children were especially good, she broke off pieces for them. Many people still enjoy Wild Raspberries today; they use them to make jams and jellies. Some people say Wild Raspberries have been depleted by the overgrazing of cattle.

Blackcap
(Rose Family)

Rubus leucodermis Dougl. ex T. & G.
(Rosaceae)

Other Names: Black Raspberry, "Blackberry" (but this is more generally applied to *Rubus ursinus*), "Wild Loganberry".

Botanical Description

Blackcap is a raspberry-like shrub with long, arching branches and numerous recurved prickles along the stems. The bark is smooth and greenish to purplish, but covered with a thick, waxy coating that gives it a characteristic blue-grey cast. The leaves, prickly veined and white beneath, are compound, like raspberry leaves, consisting of two lateral leaflets and a large terminal one, all sharply toothed. The flowers are white and often clustered. The berries are similar to raspberries, but are purplish-black, shorter and finer. When ripe, they fall off readily. To many people, the berries are sweet and juicy, but some find them bland and seedy. The quality of berries varies greatly with location and ripening conditions.

Habitat: open woods, clearings and burns.

Distribution in British Columbia: throughout the southern part of the province, generally south of 51°N latitude.

Aboriginal Use

Blackcap berries were – and still are – a common food of the Stl'atl'imx, Nlaka'pamux, Okanagan, Secwepemc and probably others within the range of the plant. They ripen in June and July and are especially plentiful about three years after a forest fire. Today, people freeze or can them, or make jam with them; but in the old days, they mashed them and dried the pulp in cakes, as they did wild raspberries. Later, they soaked the berry cakes in water and ate them as a dessert, or mixed them with dried meat or fish as a type of pemmican. It is said that fruit from some localities is watery and tasteless, while other areas yield sweet and flavourful berries. The Lower Nlaka'pamux used to peel and eat the young shoots in the spring, like Thimbleberry shoots.

Blackcaps in a cedar-root basket.
(Courtesy of Edith O'Donaghey.)

Thimbleberry
(Rose Family)

Rubus parviflorus Nutt.
(Rosaceae)

Botanical Description
Thimbleberry is an erect, many-stemmed shrub 1 to 2 metres tall. The bark is light brown, thin and shredded. The leaves are large and light green, resembling maple leaves with five pointed lobes; they have toothed edges and fine fuzz on both sides. The flowers are large and white, growing in terminal clusters of a few to many. The berries turn from green to whitish to pink to bright red as they ripen. They are shallowly cup shaped and, when ripe, fall easily from their stems. Their flavour varies with locality and weather conditions, but ideally, they are sweet and tasty.

Habitat: open woods, clearings and along roadsides, often forming dense thickets.

Distribution in British Columbia: widespread south of latitude 55°N; common along the coast north to Haida Gwaii.

Aboriginal Use

Thimbleberries ripen in June and July. The Sekani and all aboriginal groups of the central and southern interior ate them – and they are still very popular. Some people consider Thimbleberries superior in flavour to Wild Raspberries and wild strawberries. Unfortunately, Thimbleberries are so soft and juicy they are difficult to pick, so they were seldom gathered in large enough quantities to be dried for winter storage. Sometimes people mixed them with Wild Raspberries or Blackcaps. Like many coastal peoples, the Nlaka'pamux peeled and ate young Thimbleberry shoots in spring, either raw or cooked with meat in a stew. People often used the large, maple-like leaves as temporary containers, liners for baskets, separators for different kinds of berries in the same basket and as a surface for drying berries. The Ulkatcho Carrier, Secwepemc and probably other groups use Thimbleberry leaves to line their roasting pits both to protect the food being cooked and to add flavour to it.

Black Cottonwood	*Populus balsamifera* **L.**
ssp. *trichocarpa* **(T. & G. ex Hook.) Brayshaw**	
Balsam Poplar	*P. balsamifera* **L. ssp.** *balsamifera*
Trembling Aspen	*P. tremuloides* **Michx.**
(Willow Family)	**(Salicaceae)**

Other Names: Poplar; Northern Black Cottonwood (ssp. *trichocarpa*); White Poplar (*P. tremuloides*).

Botanical Description

Black Cottonwood and Balsam Poplar are rough-barked trees, up to 50 metres tall, with resinous, sweet-smelling spring buds and leaves. The leaves are long-stemmed and generally heart-shaped, triangular or more oval, with wedge-shaped bases. The leaf tips are sharply pointed and the margins finely toothed. In Spring the leaves are characteristically yellow-green and the buds are fragrant. The flowers are long, pendulant catkins, male and female being on separate trees. At fruiting-time, the female catkins are covered with a soft, downy cotton-like substance, which is released with the seeds in mid summer, filling the air with bits of white fluff resembling snowflakes. Black Cottonwood has thick, leathery leaves and hairy fruit capsules; Balsam Poplar has thinner leaves and smooth fruit capsules. They often hybridize, but some botanists treat them as distinct species: *Populus trichocarpa* and *P. balsamifera.* Trembling Aspen is smaller, and more slender, with smooth whitish bark and round, abruptly pointed, long-stemmed leaves that flutter in the wind. In older trees the branches are concentrated toward the top, the lower trunk being bare for 6 metres or more.

Black Cottonwood.

Habitat: Black Cottonwood and Balsam Poplar are found along watercourses, in gullies and on floodplains – both are able to withstand periodic flooding; Trembling Aspen is common in open meadows and woods and mixed coniferous forest.

Distribution in British Columbia: Black Cottonwood is found at low and high elevations throughout the province, except in the extreme northeast and Haida Gwaii, intergrading with Balsam Poplar where their ranges overlap; Balsam Poplar occurs across northern British Columbia from the Peace River to the Yukon; and Trembling Aspen is common throughout the interior and occurs sporadically on the coast and Vancouver Island.

Aboriginal Use

Poplar cambium was eaten by peoples in several parts of the interior. Black Cottonwood cambium was the most widely used, but cambium from Balsam Poplar and Trembling Aspen was also eaten by some. The Ktunaxa, Okanagan and Secwepemc ate poplar cambium only rarely, whereas the Stl'atl'imx, Dene-thah, Sekani and the Flathead of Montana considered it a great delicacy and ate it in large quantities. Cambium is ready to harvest in May in the southern part of the province and in June and July in the north. People often peeled off a test strip to see whether the cambium of a particular tree was sweet and ripe for harvesting. No aboriginal groups attempted to dry it for storage, but only ate it while fresh and succulent. Cottonwood cambium is said to ferment quickly after being harvested, so it was best to eat it fresh.

APPENDIX 1

Coastal Food Plants

Some food plants used by First Peoples of the coast were also used by interior peoples, but only peripherally or sporadically. These species are described in detail in *Food Plants of Coastal First Peoples* (Turner 1995). Here are brief discussions of their significance to interior aboriginal groups. They are listed in the same general order as the plants in the main text.

Red Laver   *Porphyra abbottae* **Krishnamurthy**
(or Edible Seaweed)   **and other *Porphyra* species**
Red Algae   **Rhodophyceae**

Red Laver was commonly dried and eaten by coastal First Peoples. The Nisga'a, whose territory extends to the coast in one area, gathered Red Laver on the north side of Portland Canal and also frequently obtained it by trade. They dried it in the sun and chopped it into pieces, "like corn flakes", for storage; a handful, boiled up, would feed three or four people. Red Laver is still a popular food among the Nisga'a. The Carrier and Tsilhqot'in sometimes obtained dried Red Laver from the Nuxalk, who obtained it through trade from the Heiltsuk on the outer coast. The Gitxsan, Wet'suwet'en and other interior groups also obtained seaweed through trade. Interior peoples sometimes ate seaweed to combat goitre, an affliction caused by iodine deficiency. The Nisga'a used other sea plants, such as Giant Kelp and Eelgrass, to collect herring spawn.

Spiny Wood Fern	*Dryopteris expansa* (K.B. Presl)
	Fraser-Jenkins & Jermy
Licorice Fern	*Polypodium glycyrrhiza* D.C. Eat.
Sword Fern	*Polystichum munitum* (Kaulf.) Presl
Fern Family	Polypodiaceae

The Lower Stl'atl'imx of the Pemberton area dug up the fleshy root-stocks of Spiny Wood Fern in the fall and early spring, then roasted, peeled and ate them. The Nisga'a, Gitxsan and Wet'suwet'en also ate the rootstocks, which they dug up early in the spring and roasted in earth ovens. The Lower Stl'atl'imx and Lower Nlaka'pamux chewed the rhizomes of Licorice Fern, especially for colds and sore throats. The Lower Nlaka'pamux of the Spuzzum area used to eat the rhizomes of Sword Fern.

| Western Hemlock | *Tsuga heterophylla* (Raf.) Sarg. |
| Pine Family | Pinaceae |

The Nisga'a scraped off the cambium from Western Hemlock trees, baked it in earth ovens, formed it into cakes and ate it fresh or dried, as did many coastal groups. It has a sweetish taste. A favourite way to prepare the dried cambium was to whip it with snow and Eulachon grease. Nisga'a people still consider this a good food, but rarely make it nowadays. Wet'suwet'en and Gitxsan people also ate Western Hemlock cambium when it was available.

| Wapato (or Arrow-head) | *Sagittaria latifolia* Wild. |
| Water Plaintain Family | Alismataceae |

The Lower Nlaka'pamux of the Spuzzum area once acquired the edible tubers of Wapato from the Halkomelem people of the Fraser River valley, carrying them up the canyon in large baskets. They steamed the tubers in pits or boiled them like potatoes. Wapato and a related species, *Sagittaria cuneata*, also grow in the interior, but people within their range did not usually eat the tubers, except for some Secwepemc people who gathered them. The extent to which interior people used Wapato needs further study. These plants are said to be much less common than they used to be, because of the pressures of development and the impact of cattle grazing in wetlands.

Wapato.

Rice Root   *Fritillaria camschatcensis*
(or Mission Bells)   **(L.) Ker-Gawl.**
Lily Family   **Liliaceae**
The Nisga'a, Gitxsan and Wet'suwet'en boiled and ate the rice-like bulbs and bulblets of Rice Root, as did many coastal aboriginal groups. The Gitxsan's use of Rice Root is described in detail in *Gathering What the Great Nature Provided* ('Ksan 1980).

Calypso   *Calypso bulbosa* **(L.) Oakes**
Orchid Family   **Orchidaceae**
The Lower Stl'atl'imx of the Pemberton area ate the small, white corms of Calypso raw after peeling them. The Stl'atl'imx name for Calypso means "easily peeled". The Sekani and possibly other northern peoples also ate them as a snack or treat.

Note: Calypso is a beautiful orchid, and uncommon in many localities. Do not sample the corms – digging one up destroys the entire plant.

Broad-leaved Maple   *Acer macrophyllum* **Pursh**
Maple Family   **Aceraceae**
The Lower Nlaka'pamux of the Spuzzum area gathered the young shoots of Broad-leaved Maple when they were about 3 cm tall, and peeled and ate them raw. They also boiled and ate the sprouted seeds.

Bunchberry   *Cornus canadensis* L.
(or Dwarf Dogwood)
Dogwood Family   Cornaceae

Many coastal groups ate the fruit of the Bunchberry; but of the interior peoples, apparently only the Lower Stl'atl'imx of the Pemberton area, the Wet'suwet'en and the Sekani ate them. The Carrier thought them to be good for birds and bears. The Ktunaxa recognized them, but did not believe them to be edible.

Stonecrop   *Sedum divergens* Wats.
Orpine Family   Crassulaceae

The Nisga'a, Wet'suwet'en and the Stl'atl'imx of the Mount Currie - Pemberton area ate the fleshy red leaves of Stonecrop raw, as did the Haida. They ate them before the plants flowered in the spring. The Nisga'a usually served Stonecrop leaves with Eulachon grease and sugar. Many people considered Stonecrop a good dessert after a fish dinner, because it leaves a sweet aftertaste.

Salal   *Gaultheria shallon* Pursh
Heather Family   Ericaceae

The Lower Nlaka'pamux of the Spuzzum area ate Salal berries when available; they usually mashed and dried them in cakes. The Lower Stl'atl'imx sometimes obtained them by trade. Salal berries are rare in Nisga'a territory and apparently were not used much there.

Alaska Blueberry   *Vaccinium alaskaense* Howell
Heather Family   Ericaceae

The range of Alaska Blueberry extends into the territories of the Lower Nlaka'pamux and Lower Stl'atl'imx, who ate the fruits, fresh or dried, as they did other types of blueberries.

Evergreen Huckleberry　　　　　　　*Vaccinium ovatum* **Pursh**
Heather Family　　　　　　　　　　　　　**Ericaceae**
According to E. Steedman in "Ethnobotany of the Thompson Indians of British Columbia" (1930), the Nlaka'pamux gathered the sweet, reddish-black berries of Evergreen Huckleberry. But the range of this plant is generally restricted to the coast, so their availability to the Nlaka'pamux is doubtful.

Red Huckleberry　　　　　　　　*Vaccinium parvifolium* **Sm.**
Heather Family　　　　　　　　　　　　　**Ericaceae**
The Lower Nlaka'pamux, Lower Stl'atl'imx, Nisga'a, eastern Secwepemc and possibly the Ktunaxa ate Red Huckleberries fresh or dried. They prepared them in similar ways to blueberries and Mountain Bilberry.

Indian Plum　　　　　　　　　　*Oemleria cerasiformis*
　　　　　　　　　　　　(T. & G. ex Hook. & Arn.) Landon
Rose Family　　　　　　　　　　　　　　**Rosaceae**
The Lower Nlaka'pamux of the Spuzzum area called Indian Plum by the same name as Saskatoon Berry, although they knew it to be different. They regarded the berries as edible, but believed that if you ate too many your lungs would bleed. (*Oemlaria cerasiformis* was formerly known as *Osmaronia cerasiformis*.)

Wild Crabapple　　　　　　　　　　　*Pyrus fusca* **Raf.**
Rose Family　　　　　　　　　　　　　　**Rosaceae**
The Lower Nlaka'pamux, Lower Stl'atl'imx and Nisga'a ate Wild Crabapples, as did many groups on the coast. The Nisga'a boiled and mixed them with oil for storage; in winter, they mixed the crabapples with snow and whipped in Eulachon grease to make a treat like ice cream. (*Pyrus fusca* is also called *Malus fusca* or *Malus diversifolia*.)

Salmonberry   *Rubus spectabilis* **Pursh**
Rose Family   **Rosaceae**
The Lower Nlaka'pamux, Lower Stl'atl'imx, Wet'suwet'en and Nisga'a
ate Salmonberries whenever available. They ate them fresh, but seldom dried them. The Lower Nlaka'pamux also peeled and ate the
young shoots in spring, like those of Thimbleberry.

Trailing Wild Blackberry   *Rubus ursinus* **Cham. & Schlecht.**
Rose Family   **Rosaceae**
The Lower Nlaka'pamux and Lower Stl'atl'imx ate the fruit of Trailing
Wild Blackberry, although in both areas the plant is restricted to a few
localities. Both groups have mythical traditions tracing the origin of the
wild blackberry vine to the blood of a young woman who was stranded
up a tree by her jealous husband.

Sitka Mountain-ash   *Sorbus sitchensis* **Roemer**
Rose Family   **Rosaceae**
The Lower Stl'atl'imx, Lower Nlaka'pamux and Okanagan occasionally ate the berries of Sitka Mountain-ash, but other interior groups did
not eat them at all, according to available information. Recently, the
Lower Nlaka'pamux cooked them with turkey and other meat. A cluster of Sitka Mountain-ash berries added to a jar of canned blueberries
is said to give the preserves a pleasant, tart flavour.

Stinging Nettle   *Urtica dioica* **L.**
Nettle Family   **Urticaceae**
The Southern Okanagan, the Upper Stl'atl'imx of the Fraser River and
some other interior peoples ate the young leaves and stems of Stinging
Nettle, but this practice may have been learned from Europeans.
Before eating the greens, they boiled them for a short time to eliminate
their stinging properties.

APPENDIX 2

Casual Edibles, Tea and Tobacco

Interior First Peoples used these plants in limited amounts or sporadically as sources of tea, tobacco, gum, casual edibles and flower nectar.

Black Spruce *Picea mariana* **(Mill.) B.S.P.**
Pine Family **Pinaceae**
Black Spruce is confined to cold swamps or bogs of northern British Columbia. The Carrier, Dene-thah, Sekani and possibly other Athapaskan groups chewed the pitch for pleasure. Many interior peoples also chewed the pitch of White Spruce.

White Pine *Pinus monticola* **Dougl. ex D. Don**
Pine Family **Pinaceae**
The Nlaka'pamux collected White Pine gum and chewed it for pleasure. The Secwepemc sliced and ate the green cones. They taste pitchy and strong, but not bitter. Nevertheless, it was said that a "good" (strong) man could eat no more than two slices. The Flathead Salish of Montana ate the cambium, and removed and ate the seeds from partially roasted cones.

Milkweed *Asclepias speciosa* **Torr.**
Milkweed Family **Asclepiadaceae**
As a food, Milkweed should be regarded with caution – it contains bitter alkaloids. But the Crow people of Montana boiled and ate the flowers and also ate the raw seeds from immature pods. The Flathead of Montana, and the Cheyenne, Secwepemc and Okanagan chewed the coagulated latex for pleasure.

Dwarf Birch
Birch Family

Betula glandulosa **Michx.**
Betulaceae

Tsilhqot'in and possibly other peoples made tea from the leaves and twigs of Dwarf Birch.

Hooker's Fairy Bells
Rough-fruited Fairy Bells
Lily Family

Disporum hookeri **(Torrey) Nichols.**
D. trachycarpum **(Wats.) B. & H.**
Liliaceae

Most interior First Peoples did not eat the berries of these herbaceous perennials; the Ktunaxa called them "Grizzly Bear's favourite food" (the name they also gave to Twisted Stalk and False Solomon's Seal) and did not believe them to be edible. But some Nlaka'pamux and Secwepemc people ate them raw. One Nlaka'pamux woman called Hooker's Fairy Bells "tomato plant", because the berries resemble miniature tomatoes.

Long-flowered Stoneseed
Borage Family

Lithospermum incisum **Lehm.**
Boraginaceae

The Nlaka'pamux name for Long-flowered Stoneseed means "bloody", in reference to the red-staining roots. According to L.J. Clark (1973), one of its other common names, Puccoon, is derived from an Algonkian term for plants used for staining and dyeing. The Nlaka'pamux used to eat the large, deep taproots cooked, but have not used them for many years. The Secwepemc used the roots to make a red paint; they also made a tea to improve the appetite from the roots of a related species, *L. ruderale*.

Orange Honeysuckle
Honeysuckle Family

Lonicera ciliosa **(Pursh) DC.**
Caprifoliaceae

Lower Stl'atl'imx children at Pemberton, as well as children in other groups, used to suck the nectar from Orange Honeysuckle flowers. No one ate the berries.

Red Twinberry
Honeysuckle Family

Lonicera utahensis **Wats.**
Caprifoliaceae

Okanagan hunters sometimes ate Red Twinberries, which were said to be a good emergency source of water because they are so juicy. Apparently, the Ktunaxa and Stl'atl'imx did not eat them.

Silverberry *Elaeagnus commutata* **Bernh. ex Rydb.**
Oleaster Family **Elaeagnaceae**
The Nlaka'pamux and Okanagan occasionally ate Silverberries fresh or dried, although they are dry and astringent.

Pipsissewa *Chimaphila umbellata* **(L.) Bart.**
(or Prince's Pine)
Heather family **Ericaceae**
The Nlaka'pamux boiled leaves, stems and roots of Pipsissewa to make a tea. The Lower Stl'atl'imx and other groups also made a tea from Pipsissewa, but only for colds and sore throats. The Flathead of Montana smoked the leaves.

Licorice Root or Sweet Vetch *Hedysarum alpinum* **L.**
Bean Family **Fabaceae**
Sekani elders recall eating a sweet type of wild root that they call "Grizzly Bear root", apparently this species. They dug it up in the mountains and ate it raw or dried it for winter. They note that bears like to eat it, too, early in the spring.

Canada Mint *Mentha arvensis* **L.**
Mint Family **Lamiaceae or Labiatae**
The Secwepemc, Nlaka'pamux, Okanagan, Ktunaxa, Sekani and other interior groups used Canada Mint leaves, fresh or dried, for tea. The tea could be used as a beverage or, in stronger doses, as a medicine for colds, coughs, consumption and fever. Many people still drink mint tea today. The Ktunaxa also sprinkled powdered mint leaves on cooked meat as a flavouring, especially if the meat was fatty; this probably helped to preserve it, also.

Wild Bergamot
Mint Family
Monarda fistulosa **L.**
Lamiaceae or Labiatae

The Ktunaxa called Wild Bergamot "dry-land mint", as opposed to Canada Mint, which they called "water mint". They used Wild Bergamot leaves in the same way, fresh or dried, steeped in hot water to make

a refreshing tea. Some Secwepemc people also burned this plant as a smudge against mosquitoes. The Kalispel and Spokane peoples of Washington used a related species, *Monardella odoratissima*, to make an aromatic tea.

Self-heal (or Heal-all)
Mint Family
Prunella vulgaris **L.**
Lamiaceae or Labiatae

James Teit noted that the Nlaka'pamux soaked Self-heal in cold water to make "one of the most common drinks of the Indians" (Steedman 1930) and that it was often used as a tonic by local European settlers. But I could find no recent evidence of its use as a beverage by aboriginal peoples.

Buckbrush
Snowbush
Buckthorn Family
Ceanothus sanguineus **Pursh**
C. velutinus **Dougl. ex Hook.**
Rhamnaceae

The Ktunaxa and some Interior Salish used the leaves of Snowbush and Buckbrush to make a tea, which was said to be a good medicine; the leaves were also used as a simple beverage. Both plants are related to New Jersey Tea of eastern North America.

Purple Avens   *Geum triflorum* **Pursh**
(or Old Man's Whiskers)
Rose Family   **Rosaceae**
Nlaka'pamux and Okanagan people boiled or steeped the roots of
Purple Avens to make a tea for use as a beverage or appetizer and also
as a medicine for colds, flu and fever.

Cinquefoil   *Potentilla glandulosa* **Lindl.**
Rose Family   **Rosaceae**
The Nlaka'pamux boiled the entire Cinquefoil plant or just the leaves
to make a tea, which is said to be a mild stimulant.

Spiraea   *Spiraea pyramidata* **Greene**
Rose Family   **Rosaceae**
The Nlaka'pamux and Sekani, and possibly other peoples, made a tea
by boiling the stems, leaves and flowers of Spiraea.

Bastard Toadflax   *Comandra umbellata* **(L.) Nutt.**
Sandalwood Family   **Santalaceae**
Okanagan children reportedly sucked the nectar from Bastard Toadflax
flowers. Stl'atl'imx people sometimes ate the berries.

Alum-root   *Heuchera cylindrica* **Dougl. ex Hook.**
Saxifrage Family   **Saxifragaceae**
The Stl'atl'imx, Okanagan and Ktunaxa used Alum-root leaves for tea.
Apparently, the Stl'atl'imx drank it as a beverage; the others used the
tea as a medicine or tonic. The astringent roots make a well-known
poultice for mouth sores, boils and skin infections.

Mountain Valerian   *Valeriana dioica* **L. and** *V. sitchensis* **Bong.**
Valerian Family   **Valerianaceae**
Some Nlaka'pamux men mixed the dried powdered roots and leaves
of Mountain Valerian with tobacco as a flavouring. (Photograph on
next page.)

Edible Valerian *Valeriana edulis* **Nutt. ex T. & G.**
Valerian Family **Valerianaceae**

The large sweet-tasting taproots of Edible Valerian were steamed and eaten by the Southern Okanagan groups, as well as by the Kalispel and Spokane of Washington and the Flathead of Montana. To some people they were a favourite food, but others noted that they have a strong, unpleasant smell.

Mountain Valerian
(*Valeriana sitchensis*).

APPENDIX 3

Some Non-Native Food Plants
Used by Interior First Peoples

Onions   *Allium cepa* **L.**
Lily Family   Liliaceae
Onions have been imported and cultivated by the southern interior peoples since the late 1800s. In aboriginal languages, they are usually named after wild Nodding Onions. The Stl'atl'imx word for cultivated onions is simply "onions" and their word for Nodding Onions means "real onions".

Rice   *Oryza sativa* **L.**
Grass Family   Poaceae or Gramineae
Interior First Peoples acquired rice as a trade good fairly early in the history of their contact with Europeans, and it has long been a popular food in some areas of the interior. The Nlaka'pamux name for it is translated literally as "Chinaman's food", and the Ktunaxa name means "resembling maggots".

Carrots   *Daucus carota* **L.**
Parsnips   *Pastinaca sativa* **L.**
Celery Family   Apiaceae or Umbelliferae
Since the late 1800s, interior First Peoples have used and cultivated carrots and parsnips. In some Interior Salish languages, cultivated carrots are named after wild counterparts, such as Desert Parsley or Wild Caraway. In the Lower Stl'atl'imx language, parsnips are associated with Sweet Cicely ("dry-land parsnips") and Water Parsnips ("swamp parsnips").

Sunflower
Aster Family

Helianthus annuus **L.**
Asteraceae or Compositae

James Teit noted that sunflower seeds were introduced fairly recently to the Nlaka'pamux area and, as of 1920, were eaten in fairly large quantities by Nlaka'pamux children (Steedman 1930). Montana First Peoples ate the seeds of the wild *H. annuus*; they boiled or scorched them, pounded them into meal and made cakes with the meal. In Interior Salish languages, sunflower seeds are often called by the same name as those of Balsamroot.

Pineapple Weed
Aster Family

Matricaria matricarioides **(Less.) Porter**
Asteraceae or Compositae

According to one source, Okanagan children used to eat the flower heads of Pineapple Weed. The Flathead Salish of Montana dried and sprinkled them over drying meat and fruit to keep flies away. The Ktunaxa and Stl'atl'imx did not eat them, but some people hung the plants up as an air freshener and used them to stuff pillows because of their nice smell. (*Matricaria matricarioides* is also known as *M. discoidea*.)

Common Dandelion
Aster Family

Taraxacum officinale **Weber**
Asteraceae or Compositae

This well-known weed was introduced from Europe, probably around the mid 1800s. The Carrier, Sekani, Okanagan and other peoples soon learned about the edibility of dandelion leaves. They harvested them in spring, and boiled and ate them as greens. People also knew of the use of dandelion flowers in wine making.

Turnips
Mustard Family

Brassica rapa **L.**
Brassicaceae or Cruciferae

Aboriginal peoples commonly cultivated turnips within the last century, especially around Merritt. The Nlaka'pamux called yellow turnips "yellow head" and white turnips "white head little-flattened-behind turnip".

Shepherd's Purse *Capsella bursa-pastoris* **L.**
Mustard Family **Brassicaceae or Cruciferae**
Shepherd's Purse is a common edible garden weed with a peppery, cabbage-like flavour. Some Nlaka'pamux people soaked the leaves in salted water and ate them as a green vegetable.

Watercress *Rorippa nasturtium-aquaticum* **(L.) Hayek**
Mustard Family **Brassicaceae or Cruciferae**
Early prospectors and pioneers introduced Watercress into streams and other watercourses throughout the province to provide a source of fresh greens. Today, aboriginal peoples such as the Okanagan, Secwepemc and Stl'atl'imx eat it raw. But some Flathead people of Montana cook and eat it like spinach.

Beets *Beta vulgaris* **L.**
Goosefoot Family **Chenopodiaceae**
Beets were sometimes cultivated, at least by the Nlaka'pamux and Okanagan, within the last century.

Lamb's Quarters *Chenopodium album* **L.**
(or Pigweed)
Goosefoot Family **Chenopodiaceae**
A common garden and barnyard weed, Lamb's Quarters was apparently introduced from Eurasia (although aboriginal peoples of eastern North America cultivated similar species indigenous to this continent for their greens and seeds). The Stl'atl'imx, Okanagan, Secwepemc and Flathead of Montana boiled and ate the plants as greens. Farther south, the Cheyenne and other groups pounded the seeds into flour, along with Sunflower seeds, to make bread.

Sweet Potatoes　　　　　　　　　　*Ipomoea batatas* (L.) Lam.
Bindweed Family　　　　　　　　　　Convolvulaceae
Aboriginal peoples in British Columbia did not cultivate Sweet Potatoes within the last century, but they did eat them. A number of wild edible roots, including Yellow Avalanche Lily and Silverweed are now called "wild sweet potatoes" by some aboriginal people. The Kalispel name for Sweet Potato is the same as the name for "Wild Carrot".

Melons　　　　　　　　　　　　*Cucumis melo* L.
　　　　　　　　　　and *Citrullus vulgaris* Schrad.
Cucumber Family　　　　　　　　　　Cucurbitaceae
Cantaloupes, watermelons and honeydew melons are all highly regarded by the southern interior First Peoples, especially the Nlaka'pamux and Okanagan, as well as by the Flathead and other aboriginal groups in the United States. Since the early 1900s, many people have grown melons in their gardens. (*Citrullus vulgaris* is also known as *C. lanatus.*)

Squash and Pumpkin　　　　　　　　*Cucurbita pepo* L.
Cucumber Family　　　　　　　　　　Cucurbitaceae
The Nlaka'pamux, Okanagan and other interior peoples have cultivated squash and pumpkin since the late 1800s. Nlaka'pamux children liked to eat the seeds.

Beans　　　　　　　　　　　　*Phaseolus vulgaris* L.
Peas　　　　　　　　　　　　　*Pisum sativum* L.
Pea Family　　　　　　　　Fabaceae or Leguminosae
Most interior First Peoples have grown and eaten beans and peas, obtaining them initially from early European pioneers and traders. The Okanagan name for peas is *lipuwa*, from the French, *le pois*.

Currants and Gooseberries　　　　　　　*Ribes* spp.
Gooseberry Family　　　　　　　　　Grossulariaceae
Several varieties of cultivated currants and gooseberries were – and still are – cultivated in the gardens of interior First Peoples. They were generally named after their wild counterparts.

Rhubarb   *Rheum rhabarbarum* L.
Knotweed Family   **Polygonaceae**
Rhubarb is popular among interior First Peoples and has been commonly cultivated within the last century. Almost all interior peoples as-
sociate it with Cow Parsnip, which is called "Wild Rhubarb" or "Indian
Rhubarb" by many people. Garden rhubarb is usually given the same
aboriginal name as Cow Parsnip.

Sour-grass (or Sheep Sorrel)   *Rumex acetosella* L.
Knotweed Family   **Polygonaceae**
A low weed of gardens and waste places, Sour-grass was introduced
from Europe. The Nlaka'pamux, and possibly some other interior
peoples, chewed the raw leaves as a snack. A recently devised Nlaka'pamux name for it translates as "sour ground growth".

Tree Fruits:
  Peaches, Cherries and Plums   *Prunus* spp.
  Apples   *Malus* spp.
  Pears   *Pyrus* spp.
Rose Family   **Rosaceae**
All of these fruits, when introduced, were grown and eaten by interior
First Peoples, especially those in the south. Cultivated cherries were
often equated with Choke Cherries. Some Ktunaxa people are fond of
cultivated crabapples. They call them by the same name as Kinnik-
innick berries, because they are similar in taste and texture.

Raspberries   *Rubus idaeus* L.
Strawberries   *Fragaria* spp.
Rose Family   **Rosaceae**
Many interior First Peoples have cultivated raspberries and strawber-
ries within the last century. These berries are usually named after their
wild counterparts.

Mullein   *Verbascum thapsus* L.
Figwort Family   **Scrophulariaecae**
Since its introduction from Eurasia, Mullein has become a common
weed in the southern interior. Some aboriginal people call it "Wild

Tobacco". Annie York, a Nlaka'pamux woman from Spuzzum, said that aboriginal people used to smoke the leaves, but warned that the smoke could be poisonous if too much were inhaled. The Ktunaxa people made their horses inhale the smoke to clear their nostrils if they were plugged up due to a cold.

Tomatoes *Lycopersicon esculentum* **Mill.**
Potato Family **Solanaceae**
First Peoples of the southern interior have cultivated Tomatoes since the late 1800s. The Nlaka'pamux name for them is *temáytus*, a direct borrowing from English. The Okanagan call them by the same name as rose hips.

Tobacco *Nicotiana* **spp.**
Potato Family **Solanaceae**
The Nlaka'pamux, Okanagan, Secwepemc and Ktunaxa originally cultivated and smoked Wild Tobacco; so did the Coeur d'Alene and Flathead Salish of Idaho and Montana, among other groups. It may also have been gathered in the wild state, but indications are that it persisted only under cultivation. Tobacco Plains, in Ktunaxa territory on the British Columbia - Montana border, was named after the large quantities of Wild Tobacco once grown here. There were various ways of preparing it for smoking, the most common being to gather and dry the leaves after the plants flowered, then toast and grease them to keep them from getting too dry. Smoking mixtures were often made by adding such materials as dried Kinnikinnick leaves, Mountain Valerian roots and leaves, Dwarf Wild Rose leaves and bark, Red Osier Dogwood leaves, huckleberry or blueberry leaves, or "Indian Marijuana" (Canby's Lovage) leaves. People smoked these mixtures in carved pipes of wood and stone. The Nisga'a and Tahltan obtained a native tobacco from the Haida, Tlingit and Coast Tsimshian through trade; tentatively identified as a variety of *N. quadrivalvis*, this tobacco was not smoked but chewed with pine bark or lime from burnt shells.

When commercial tobacco (Common Tobacco) was introduced by European traders it was quickly adopted by aboriginal people and use of the native tobaccos was generally discontinued. Even those groups who did not smoke originally, such as the Carrier and Tsilhqot'in, soon

learned to smoke the new tobacco. Commercial tobacco, like native tobacco, was often mixed with Kinnikinnick and other wild plants to improve its taste and make it last longer. According to James Teit, the first
commercial tobacco to be smoked by First Peoples was some "black
twist" given to the Secwepemc by Simon Fraser. It apparently made
many of them sick. Among the Secwepemc, tobacco (not necessarily
Nicotiana) was an important guardian spirit; its role in mythical times
was as a cannibal tree that killed anyone who touched its leaves or
rested in its shade.

Potatoes   *Solanum tuberosum* L.
Potato Family   Solanaceae
Potatoes were extremely important as a crop plant to the interior First
Peoples of the province, as they were to coastal peoples. They were one
of the first cultivated plants introduced to aboriginal peoples and even
today are an important vegetable. They were introduced to the Nisga'a
in the Upper Nass villages in 1859, and are still harvested there. But the
Tahltan and other Athapaskan groups of the far north had little success
trying to cultivate them because of the severity of the weather. The
groups of the southern interior generally associated potatoes with various wild edible roots such as Spring Beauty, and the Lower Nlaka'pamux associated them with Wapato. They sometimes named potatoes
after these plants.

APPENDIX 4

Some Plants Considered Poisonous or Inedible by Interior First Peoples

Queenscup
Lily Family

Clintonia uniflora (Schult.) Kunth
Liliaceae

Queenscup is a low herbaceous plant that grows in shaded montane forests in the southern two-thirds of the province. The leaves, usually two per plant, are basal and *Erythronium*-like, tapering at each end. The flower is white and solitary on a slender stem, producing a single bright-blue berry. This plant is not well known to contemporary aboriginal people, but both the Lower Stl'atl'imx and Lower Nlaka'pamux believed the berry to be inedible. The former used it as an eye medicine, the latter as a blue dye.

Mountain Bells
Lily Family

Stenanthium occidentale A. Gray
Liliaceae

Mountain Bells is a slender herbaceous plant that grows in damp, shaded woods in the southern part of the province, especially along the

 coast and in the Rocky Mountain Trench. The leaves are tapering and grass-like. The flowers are small, greenish or brownish purple, and drooping in an erect, long-stemmed cluster. Some Nlaka'pamux people believed the entire plant to be highly poisonous to both humans and animals – especially the bulbs, which are elongated and tapering. They consider Mountain Bells a close relative of the poisonous False Hellebore, which is also in the Lily Family (see page 180).

Queenscup (above) and
Twisted Stalk (right).

Twisted Stalk   *Streptopus amplexifolius* (L.) DC.
and *S. streptopoides* (Ledeb.) Frye & Rigg
Lily Family   **Liliaceae**
These closely related species, both called Twisted Stalk, are slender
herbaceous perennials of shaded forests and stream banks. *Streptopus
amplexifolius* stems grow up to 1 metre high, usually branching below
the middle, while *S. streptopoides* stems are shorter and unbranched. The
leaves are elliptical, pointed and clasping to the stem, spaced alter-
nately along the stem, which bends slightly at each node. Small green-
ish-white or pinkish flowers are borne singly beneath each leaf along
the upper part of the stem. The fruits are elongated, red, slightly
translucent and juicy. Although James Teit reported that the Nlaka'pamux ate "great quantities" of these berries (Steedman 1930), the Stl'a-
tl'imx, Ktunaxa and other peoples believed them to be poisonous and
left them alone. The Stl'atl'imx called them "snake berries" and the
Ktunaxa called them "Grizzly Bear's favourite food", along with the
berries of False Solomon's Seal.

False Hellebore   *Veratrum viride* **Ait.**
(or Green Hellebore or Indian Hellebore)
Lily Family   **Liliaceae**
False Hellebore is a tall, robust perennial of montane meadows or, occasionally, of lowland swamps. The leaves, bright green and largest near the base of the plant, are broadly elliptical, pointed and conspicuously pleated longitudinally. Its small, green flowers are crowded in elongated terminal clusters. False Hellebore is one of the most poisonous plants in the province, a fact recognized by almost all interior First Peoples. It is well known that sheep, horses, cattle and other animals will not touch it. The poisonous principle is a combination of toxic alkaloids that act on the heart and nervous system. Some symptoms of hellebore poisoning are frothing at the mouth, lockjaw, vomiting and diarrhoea. Eating even a small portion of the plant can kill you. An aboriginal antidote is to drink a soup of boiled dried salmon heads or some other oily or greasy material, such as lard or butter.

There is at least one report of numbness of the mouth and chin, and of stomach cramps after drinking water in which False Hellebore was growing. Until more is learned of its effects in contaminating water, it

False Hellebore.   Death Camas.

is advisable not to drink water – especially stagnant or slow-running water – in the vicinity of this plant.

Despite its extreme toxicity, False Hellebore was used as a medicine by interior First Peoples, but only by those who knew exactly how to prepare it and what quantities to use. People used it externally as a blistering agent, local anaesthetic and decongestant, and internally as a physic. One Stl'atl'imx elder, who used it as a physic, noted that it opens up all the pores of the skin and you can feel the wind blow right through you. A person had to stay warm when taking this medicine, and use only the most minute quantity. Poison Hill, south of Bonaparte Lake in Secwepemc territory, and Poison Mountain in Stl'atl'imx territory are both named so because False Hellebore grows there.

Death Camas   *Zigadenus venenosus* **Wats.**
(or White Camas or "Poison Onion")
Lily Family   **Liliaceae**
Death Camas is a grass-like, bulb-bearing plant of the dry hillsides of southern British Columbia. The flowers are small and cream-coloured, and grow in a tight, pointed cluster. The bulbs resemble onions but lack the onion odour. The leaves and bulbs are extremely toxic. Death Camas is responsible for killing more sheep than any other poisonous plant within its range. Aboriginal peoples of the southern interior, including the Nlaka'pamux, Stl'atl'imx, Okanagan and Ktunaxa, were well aware of its poisonous qualities, and careful to distinguish between its bulbs and those of edible species such as Nodding Onion and Mariposa Lily. As with False Hellebore, the toxic ingredients in Death Camas are alkaloids, and the symptoms of poisoning include foaming at the mouth and lockjaw. It is said that drinking a rich fish or beef broth, or eating grease or butter, will counteract the poison. The Secwepemc say that Blue Grouse can eat the bulbs, but then their meat is poisonous to humans. Two other species found in the southern interior, *Zigadenus elegans* and *Z. gramineus*, are known to be poisonous to livestock.

Rein-orchid   *Platanthera dilatata* (Pursh) Lindl. ex Beck
(or White Bog-orchid)
Orchid Family   **Orchidaceae**

Rein-orchid is a slender, straight-stemmed herbaceous perennial with lance-shaped, upright leaves and many white, sweet-smelling flowers in an elongated terminal cluster. It is found

in bogs and wet meadows throughout the province. Some Secwepemc and Nla-ka'pamux people believe Rein-orchid to be extremely poisonous to both animals and humans. The Secwepemc used it as a poison for Coyotes and Grizzlies by boiling it and sprinkling it on bait-meat. One man was said to have lost three horses because a malicious person mixed Rein-orchid leaves with his hay. Some Nlaka'pamux people considered it a close relative of the highly poisonous False Hellebore.

Poison Ivy   *Toxidodendron radicans* (L.) Kuntze
Sumac Family   **Anacardiaceae**

Poison Ivy is a low-growing, dense shrub with compound leaves of three oval, pointed leaflets that turn red in late summer and fall. The flowers are small, greenish white and inconspicuous, and grow in clusters. The fruits are round, whitish berries. Poison Ivy grows on plains,

wastelands, moist riverbanks and talus slopes in the southern interior. Merely touching the leaves of this plant can cause a serious persistent skin rash accompanied by swelling and blistering over large areas of the body. Persons who are not affected by their first contact with Poison Ivy may become sensitized to it and incur serious injuries from further contacts with the plant. Aboriginal people are well aware of the poisonous properties of this plant, but few know of any remedies for it. The Secwepemc bathed the injured skin with the boiled tops and roots of Balsamroot or, if the whole body was affected, they inhaled the steam from this decoction. They also drank large quantities of Labrador Tea. Southern Okanagan people rubbed the affected area with the milky latex from Sumac stems, washed it with a young person's urine, or drank a tea brewed from Poison Ivy leaves. The Stl'atl'imx used an antidote they learned of from European settlers: bathing the skin with a solution of bluestone (copper sulphate). Even these measures were not very effective against severe cases of allergy. *Toxidodenron radicans* is also known as *Rhus radicans.*

Water Hemlock
Celery Family

Cicuta douglasii (DC.) Coult. & Rose
Apiaceae or Umbelliferae

Kingsbury (1964) considers *Cicuta* the most poisonous plant genus in North America. Water Hemlock is a stout herbaceous perennial, 50 to 200 cm tall, with a round, fleshy, chambered base like a small turnip. The leaves are three-times compound, with many small, narrow leaflets that are pointed and sharply toothed. An important feature of identification is that the veins on the leaflets extend to the bases of the teeth rather than to the points. The flowers are small, white and numerous, growing in flat-topped umbrella-like clusters, like those of Cow Parsnip but smaller and more slender.

Water Hemlock grows throughout British Columbia, except on Haida Gwaii, in marshes, ditches and wet low places. Almost all aboriginal people were aware of the extremely poisonous qualities of this plant – eating only a few stems or a single rootstock can kill a horse or cow. Some people recounted stories of humans poisoning themselves by confusing Water Hemlock with the edible Water Parsnip, which has a similar growth form and habitat. Symptoms of Water Hemlock poisoning are similar to those of False Hellebore poisoning: foaming at the mouth, facial distortion and lockjaw. Swallowing large amounts of oil or grease might help, but the poison works very fast. Some peoples, such as the Nlaka'pamux and Carrier, used the root as a poultice for rheumatism and other ailments, but never took it internally.

Twinflower Honeysuckle	*Lonicera involucrata*
(or Black Twinberry)	**(Rich.) Banks ex Spreng.**
Honeysuckle Family	**Caprifoliaceae**

A bushy shrub, Twinflower Honeysuckle grows up to 3 metres tall in damp, open thickets throughout the province. The leaves are dark green, paired and elliptical, tapering at both ends. The stout tubular flowers, always in twos, are subtended by broad, leafy bracts that are green at first but later turn deep red. The paired berries are black and

shiny. Nlaka'pamux, Stl'atl'imx and other peoples believed the berries to be poisonous. Some Secwepemc and Ktunaxa people did not consider them poisonous, but still did not eat them. Many interior aboriginal people call them "bear berries" or "grizzly berries" and all agree that they are a favourite food of bears.

Waxberry	*Symphoricarpos albus* **(L.) Blake**
(or Snowberry)	**and** *S. occidentalis* **Hook.**
Honeysuckle Family	**Caprifoliaceae**

Waxberries are low, bushy shrubs, often forming large thickets along roadsides and in clearings and open woods. Their paired leaves are bluish-green, rounded and occasionally lobed on young stems. The minute pinkish flowers grow in scattered clusters. The flowers of *S. albus* are compact with short petal lobes; those of *S. occidentalis* have longer, flaring petal lobes. The berries of both species are large, soft and white, sometimes remaining on the bushes well into the winter, when they are especially conspicuous.

Waxberries were not eaten by any interior aboriginal peoples. Some groups, such as the Nlaka'pamux, believed them to be fatally poisonous, and people have recounted instances of children dying from eating them. The Nlaka'pamux antidote for Waxberry poisoning is to eat large quantities of lard or grease. One Secwepemc woman recalled tasting some Waxberries with no ill effects. She said that they had no taste at all, and were light and "kind of foamy" in texture. In a number of interior aboriginal languages, Waxberries are called "corpse-berries" or "ghost-berries"; in a Stl'atl'imx narrative the berries were identified as the Saskatoon Berries of people in the Land of the Dead. Some Secwepemc and Okanagan people have seen Coyotes and deer eating them.

Strawberry Blite   *Chenopodium capitatum* (L.) Asch.
Goosefoot Family   **Chenopodiaceae**
A herbaceous annual, Strawberry Blite grows up to 80 cm tall, usually branching, with smooth green, more-or-less triangular leaves and spherical clusters of minute flowers concentrated at the ends of the branches. The flowers and fruits are brilliant red and will stain clothes and skin. It is questionable whether this plant is introduced or native. Strawberry Blite grows in open, disturbed land throughout British

Waxberry (*S. albus*).   Strawberry Blite.

Columbia. The Nlaka'pamux, Carrier and Tsilhqot'in used the flowers and fruits to make a red dye, but did not eat them. The Ktunaxa regard the round flower clusters as "berries"; some say that if you eat them you will get very fat, as if you are pregnant, and your friends will laugh at you.

Baneberry
Buttercup Family
Actaea rubra (Ait.) Willd.
Ranunculaceae

Baneberry is a tall, usually branching herbaceous perennial with large three-times compound leaves; the leaflets are oval, pointed, sharply toothed and lobed. The flowers are numerous, small and whitish, with long stamens; they are borne in elongated terminal clusters. The fruits are round, fleshy berries, usually bright red, although there is also a white-fruited form (*A. rubra* f. *neglecta*). Baneberry grows in moist, shaded woods and along stream banks across British Columbia. The berries and foliage are poisonous. The Stl'atl'imx name for the plant stems from their word for "sick". They used it sparingly as a physic and tonic boiled in water, but anyone taking it had to accept the consequences – being severely ill with nausea and digestive upset. Other contemporary aboriginal peoples consulted appeared not to recognize this plant. No one ate the berries. According to Kingsbury (1964), cases of severe *Actaea* poisoning have not been recorded in the United States, but European works cite examples of children dying after eating the berries of the European species. The toxicity of Baneberry is attributed to an essential oil, which produces symptoms of severe gastro-enteritis.

The red- and white-fruited forms of Baneberry.

Anemones
(or Wind Flowers)

Buttercup Family

Anemone cylindrica **Gray,**
A. multifida **Poir.**
and *Pulsatilla patens* **(L.) P. Mill.**
Ranunculaceae

Anemones are clumped herbaceous perennials that grow in dry open woods and prairies. The leaves are palmately divided and deeply lobed; they are mostly basal, but also grow in a tight whorl below the flower stems. The stems and foliage, especially those of *P. patens*, are densely hairy, giving the entire plant a greyish cast. The flowers of *A. cylindrica* and *A. multifida* are creamy white and fairly small (1 to 2 cm wide), whereas those of *P. patens* are mauve to purple, larger (up to 5 cm wide) and very showy. The seed heads are spherical to cylindrical woolly balls; when ripe, they break apart into a mass of cottony material to which the seeds are attached. *A. cylindrica* is found in the southern interior, *A. multifida* throughout the interior and *P. patens* in the southeast, in Ktunaxa territory.

These species, like many other members of the Buttercup Family, yield a skin-irritating compound, protoanemonin, which causes reddening, swelling, blistering and soreness upon contact. The Stl'atl'imx and Ktunaxa used the mashed leaves as counter-irritants for bruises and muscular pains, but only in small doses; if left on the affected spot for more than a few minutes, violent blistering would result, spreading over a much wider area than where the leaves were applied. Of course, the plants were never chewed or swallowed – they would blister the lips, tongue and throat. One Stl'atl'imx elder observed that wild game and livestock will not eat anemones, "even if it is the last thing in the field".

In case of poisoning or suspected poisoning from any plant, contact your local Poison Control Centre immediately.

Anemone multifida.

APPENDIX 5

Scientific Names of Plants and Animals Mentioned in this Book

Plants

Alpine Larch	*Larix lyallii*
Antelope Bush	*Purshia tridentata*
Big Sagebrush	*Artemisia tridentata*
Bluebunch Wheatgrass	*Agropyron spicatum*
Bog Rosemary	*Andromeda polifolia*
Cascara	*Rhamnus purshiana*
Common Tobacco	*Nicotiana tabacum*
Easter Lily (White Fawn Lily)	*Erythronium oregonum*
Eelgrass	*Zostera marina*
Engelmann Spruce	*Picea engelmannii*
Geyer's Onion	*Allium geyeri*
Giant Kelp	*Macrocystis integrifolia*
Giant Wild-rye	*Elymus cinereus*
Golden Currant	*Ribes aureum*
Indian Hemp	*Apocynum cannabinum*
Inky Cap	*Coprinus micaceus*
morels	*Morchella* spp.
Mules Ears	*Wyethia amplexicaulis*
New Jersey Tea	*Ceanothus americanus*
Oceanspray	*Holodiscus discolor*
Pacific Cinquefoil	*Potentilla pacifica*
Pacific Yew	*Taxus brevifolia*
Paper Birch	*Betula papyrifera*
Pinegrass	*Calamagrostis rubescens*
puffballs	*Lycoperdon* spp. and *Calvatia gigantea*
Red Alder	*Alnus rubra*
Red Bearberry	*Arctostaphylos rubra*

Red Currant	*Ribes triste*
Red-flowering Currant	*Ribes sanguineum*
Reed Canary Grass	*Phalaris arundinacea*
Rocky Mountain Maple	*Acer glabrum*
Salsify	*Tragopogon porrifolius*
Sandbar Willow	*Salix exigua*
Shrubby Penstemon	*Penstemon fruticosus*
Sticky Currant	*Ribes viscosissimum*
Stink Currant	*Ribes bracteosum*
Sumac	*Rhus glabra*
Supalpine Fir	*Abies lasiocarpa*
Swamp Laurel	*Kalmia polifolia*
Three-spot Tulip	*Calochortus apiculatus*
Tule	*Scirpus acutus*
Vine Maple	*Acer circinatum*
Water Birch	*Betula occidentalis*
Western Red-cedar	*Thuja plicata*
White Fawn Lily (Easter Lily)	*Erythronium oregonum*
White Spruce	*Picea glauca*
Wild Chives	*Allium schoenoprasum*
Wild Tobacco	*Nicotiana attenuata*
Wolf Lichen	*Letharia vulpina*
Wood Lily	*Lilium philadelphicum*
Yellow-cedar	*Chamaecyparis nootkatensis*

Animals

Black Bear	*Ursus americanus*
Blue Grouse	*Dendragapus obscurus*
Caribou	*Rangifer tarandus*
Clark's Nutcracker	*Nucifraga columbiana*
Coyote	*Canis latrans*
Elk	*Cervus elaphus*
Eulachon	*Thaleichthys pacificus*
Grizzly Bear	*Ursus arctos*
Moose	*Alces alces*
Mountain Goat	*Oreamnos americanus*
Mule Deer	*Odocoileus hemionus*

GLOSSARY

Algae (singular, alga) A large group of plants, mostly aquatic or marine, that have no true roots, stems, leaves or specialized conduction tissue; includes seaweeds.

Alkaloids A group of complex, basic chemical compounds produced by many types of plants, often severely toxic to humans and other animals. They usually occur in plants as a soluble organic acid-alkaline salt, and are almost always bitter in taste.

Annual A plant that lives only one year or season.

Axil The upper angle between a leaf and a stem.

Basal At or emerging from the base of a plant or structure.

Biennial A plant that lives only two years; flowers and fruits are usually produced only in the second year.

Bifurcated Divided into two parts or branches; forked.

Bract A modified leaf, either small and scale-like or large and petal-like.

Bulb A swollen underground bud, composed of a short stem covered with fleshy layers of leaf; e.g., an onion.

Cambium A layer of continuously dividing cells between the wood and the bark of trees and shrubs, from which new wood and bark tissues are derived.

Cap The expanded, often umbrella-like top portion of a mushroom.

Catkin A drooping, elongated cluster of minute petalless flowers, either male or female, as on willows, alders and birches.

Clasping Partially or completely surrounding a stem, as the bases of some leaves.

Compound leaf A leaf divided into two or more leaflets with a common leafstalk. A once compound leaf is divided once into two or more leaflets; a twice compound leaf has two or more leaflets that are also divided into two or more leaflets; and so on.

Cone A reproductive structure, either male or female, of certain trees, consisting of a central axis surrounded by numerous woody scales that bear the seeds or pollen; e.g., a pine cone.

Conifer Any cone-bearing tree such as pine, fir or spruce; a major group of gymnosperms.

Corm A fleshy, thickened underground stem at the base of a plant, usually more or less spherical, resembling a bulb, but solid rather than layered.

Crown The leafy or branching part of a tree.

Deciduous Refers to a plant that sheds all its leaves annually – as opposed to evergreen.

Dicotyledon Any member of a major subgroup of flowering plants (Dicotyledonae) characterized by embryos with two seed-leaves (cotyledons), net-veined leaves and flower parts in fours or fives – as opposed to Monocotyledons.

Drupelet One segment of an aggregate fruit such as a raspberry.

Evergreen Refers to a plant that keeps its green leaves throughout the year, even during the winter – as opposed to deciduous.

Family A category in the classification of plants and animals, ranking above a genus and below an order; including two or more related genera. Most family names end in "aceae."

Fern Any member of a broad division of non-flowering plants (Pteridophyta) that have true roots, stems, specialized conduction tissue and true leaves, which are usually large and compound or dissected. Ferns reproduce by spores, usually produced in sori on the lower surfaces or margins of the leaves.

Flowering plant Any member of a major group of vascular plants known as angiosperms (Magnoliophyta), characterized by having true flowers and seeds enclosed in a fruit.

Frond The leaf of a fern, often compound or finely dissected.

Fruit A ripened seed case or ovary and any associated structures that ripen with it.

Fungi (singular, fungus) A broad group of organisms, generally considered distinct from plants, lacking chlorophyll and true roots, stems and leaves; includes moulds, mildews, rusts, smuts and mushrooms. Fungi reproduce by spores.

Genus (plural, genera) The main subdivision of *family* in the classification of plants and animals, consisting of a group of closely related species. In the scientific name of an organism, the genus name is the first term, and the initial letter is always capitalized; e.g., *Pinus* is the genus name in *Pinus contorta* (Lodgepole Pine).

Gills The plate-like structures attached to the lower surface of the cap of many types of mushrooms, on which spores are formed.

Gymnosperm Any member of a major group of vascular plants (Pinophyta) characterized by having seeds or ovules that are not enclosed in a fruit but borne in cones or related structures. The conifers are an important subgroup of gymnosperms.

Haida Gwaii The Queen Charlotte Islands.

Herbaceous Not woody; having stems that die back to the ground at the end of the growing season.

Leaflet One of the units of a compound leaf.

Lichen Any member of a large group of composite organisms, each consisting of one or more algae and a fungus growing in a close relationship. Lichens are generally small, forming branching, leafy or encrusting structures on rock, wood, bark and soil.

Lobe The major division of a leaf extending about half way to the base or centre; oak and maple leaves are lobed.

Monocotyledon Any member of a major subgroup of flowering plants (Monocotyledonae) characterized by embryos with a single seed-leaf (cotyledon), parallel-veined leaves and flower parts in threes – as opposed to Dicotyledons.

Muskeg A poorly drained area with acidic soil, characterized by the presence of sphagnum, Labrador Tea and other specially adapted plants.

Node The point on a stem where one or more leaves or branches are attached.

Opposite Growing directly across from each other on a stem.

Perennial A plant that lives more than two years.

Petal Any member of the inside set of floral bracts in flowering plants; usually coloured or white and serving to attract insect or bird pollinators. Many flowers do not have true petals.

Pinnae (singular, Pinna) The primary lateral divisions of a pinnately compound leaf, such as a fern frond.

Pinnately compound Referring to a compound leaf with leaflets on either side of a central axis in a feather-like arrangement; e.g., the leaf of an elderberry.

Pinnule An ultimate leaflet of a leaf that is pinnately compound two or more times; i.e., the ultimate division of a compound pinna.

Recurved Curved or curled backward.

Rhizome A creeping underground stem, often fleshy, serving in vegetative reproduction and food storage.

Sepal Any member of the outside set of floral bracts in flowering plants; typically green and leaf-like, but sometimes brightly coloured and petal-like.

Sheath A thin covering surrounding an organ, such as the sheath of a grass leaf surrounding the stem.

Shrub A small to medium-sized woody perennial, usually with several permanent stems instead of a single trunk, like that of a tree.

Sori (singular, sorus) Clusters of spore cases on the underside of a fern frond.

Species (singular and plural) The fundamental unit in the classification of plants and animals, a subdivision of a genus; consisting of a group of organisms that have a high degree of similarity, show persistent differences from members of species in the same genus and usually interbreed only among themselves. In a scientific name, the species is designated by the second part, which is not capitalized; e.g., in *Pinus contorta* (Lodgepole Pine), *contorta* is the species designation.

Spike An elongated flower cluster, with flowers attached directly to the central stalk.

Stamen A male or pollen-bearing organ of a flower, consisting of a pollen capsule (anther) and a stalk (filament).

Talus A sloping mass of rock fragments at the base of a mountain or cliff.

Taproot A main root, growing straight downward, from which smaller branch roots grow out; e.g., a carrot.

Terminal Growing at the end of a stem or branch.

Tumpline A woven strap worn across the forehead and used to carry pack-baskets or other containers on the back.

Whorl A ring of three or more leaves or branches growing from the same point on a stem.

REFERENCES

Alexander, D., and R.G. Matson. 1987. *Report on the Potato Mountain Archaeological Project (1985).* Vancouver: Laboratory of Archaeology, University of British Columbia.

Anderson, J.R. 1925. *Trees and Shrubs, Food, Medicinal, and Poisonous Plants of British Columbia.* Victoria: King's Printer.

Bandoni, R.J., and A.F. Szczawinski. 1976. *Guide to Common Mushrooms of British Columbia.* Handbook no. 24. Victoria: British Columbia Provincial Museum.

Blankinship, J.W. 1905. *Native Economic Plants of Montana.* Montana Agricultural Experiment Station, Bulletin no. 56.

Bouchard, R., and D.I.D. Kennedy, eds. 1977. *Lillooet Stories.* Sound Heritage Series. Victoria: Queen's Printer.

Boyd, L.M. 1990. *'Utsoo and I. Si'ink'ez 'Utsoo.* (Ulkatcho and English; a children's book about Soapberries.) Anihim Lake, B.C.: Ulkatcho Publishing.

Brayshaw, T.C. 1985. *Pondweeds and Bur-reeds, and Their Relatives, of British Columbia.* Occasional Paper no. 26. Victoria: British Columbia Provincial Museum.

———. 1989. *Buttercups, Waterlilies and Their Relatives in British Columbia.* Memoir no. 1. Victoria: Royal British Columbia Museum.

———. 1996a. *Catkin-Bearing Plants of British Columbia.* Victoria: Royal British Columbia Museum.

———. 1996b. *Trees and Shrubs of British Columbia.* Royal British Columbia Museum Handbook. Vancouver: UBC Press; Victoria: Royal British Columbia Museum.

Carrier Linguistic Committee. 1973. *Hanüyeh Ghun 'Ütni-i. (Plants of Carrier Country).* Fort St James, B.C.: Carrier Linguistic Committee.

Chamberlain, A.B. 1892. Report on the Kootenay Indians of south-eastern British Columbia. *Eighth Report on the Northwestern Tribes of Canada.* British Association for the Advancement of Science. Edinburgh Meeting.

Clark, L.J. 1973. *Wild Flowers of British Columbia.* Sidney, B.C.: Gray's Publishing Ltd.

Cole, D., and B. Lockner, eds. 1989. *The Journals of George M. Dawson: British Columbia, 1875-1878.* 2 Vols. Vancouver: University of British Columbia Press.

Compton, B.D., B. Rigsby and M.L. Tarpent, eds. 1997. *Ethnobotany of the Gitksan Indians of British Columbia* by Harlan I. Smith. Mercury Series Paper 132, Canadian Ethnology Service. Hull, Quebec: Canadian Museum of Civilization.

Davidson, J. 1915. Botanical exploration of the province. Headwaters of Skoonkon, Botanie, Laluwissin, Murray and Twaal creeks, between the South Thompson and Fraser rivers. In *Second Annual Report of the Botanical Office,* Vancouver.

–––. 1919. Douglas Fir Sugar. *The Canadian Field Naturalist* 33:6-9.

–––. 1927. *Conifers, Junipers and Yew: Gymnosperms of British Columbia.* London: T. Fisher Unwin Ltd.

Davis, A.J. 1993. The traditional role of plants amongst the Sekani peoples of northeastern B.C. Unpublished directed studies project, University of Victoria, Environmental Studies and Anthropology; report for the Sekani Nation, Fletcher Challenge Canada, Finlay Forest Industries Ltd. and the Ministry of Forests.

Dawson, George W. 1891. Notes on the Shuswap people of British Columbia. In *Transactions of the Royal Society of Canada,* Section 2, Part 1, pp. 3-44.

Douglas, G.W., G.B.Straley and D. Meidinger. 1989-94. *The Vascular Plants of British Columbia.* 4 vols. Victoria: British Columbia Ministry of Forests.

Duff, W. 1964. *The Indian History of British Columbia.* Vol. 1, *The Impact of the White Man.* Anthropology in British Columbia Memoir no. 5. Victoria: Royal British Columbia Museum.

Duff, W., and M. Kew. 1973. A select bibliography of anthropology of British Columbia. Revised by F. Woodward and Laine Ruus. *B.C. Studies* 19:73-122

Emmons, G.T. 1911. *The Tahltan Indians.* Anthropological Publications, vol. 4, no. 1. Philadelphia: University of Pennsylvania.

Ford, R. 1985. *Prehistoric Food Production in North America.* University of Michigan, Museum of Anthropology, Anthropological Papers no. 75. Ann Arbor: University of Michigan.

Forests, Ministry of. 1992. *Biogeoclimatic Zones of British Columbia*. Map. Victoria: British Columbia Ministry of Forests, Research Branch.

French, D.H. 1965. Ethnobotany of the Pacific Northwest Indians. *Economic Botany* 19:4:378-382.

Fritz, G.J. 1984. Identification of cultivated Amaranth and Chenopod from rockshelter sites in northwestern Arkansas. *American Antiquity* 49:3: 558-72.

Gabriel, L. 1954. Food and medicines of the Okanakanes. In *18th Report of the Okanagan Historical Society*, compiled by Hester White. Okanagan Historical Society.

Goddard, P.E. 1916. *The Beaver Indians*. Anthropological Publications, vol. 10, part 4. New York: American Museum of Natural History.

Gottesfeld, L.M.J. 1992. The importance of bark products in aboriginal economies of northwestern British Columbia, Canada. *Economic Botany* 46:2: 148-57.

———. 1994a. Wet'suwet'en ethnobotany: traditional plant uses. *Journal of Ethnobiology* 14:2: 185-210.

———. 1994b. Aboriginal burning for vegetation management in northwest British Columbia. *Human Ecology* 22:2: 171-88.

———. 1994c. Conservation, territory and traditional beliefs: an analysis of Gitksan and Wet'suwet'en subsistence, northwest British Columbia, Canada. *Human Ecology* 22:4: 443-65.

———. 1995. The role of plant foods in traditional Wet'suwet'en nutrition. *Ecology of Food and Nutrition* 34:149-69.

Gunther, E. [1945] 1973. *Ethnobotany of Western Washington*. University of Washington Publications in Anthropology, vol. 10, no. 1. Seattle: University of Washington Press.

Hart, J. 1974. Plant taxonomy of the Salish and Kootenai Indians of western Montana. Master's thesis, University of Montana.

———. 1976. *Montana – Native Plants and Early Peoples*. Helena, Montana: The Montana Historical Society and The Montana Bicentennial Administration.

Hayden, B. 1992. *Complex Cultures of the British Columbia Plateau: Traditional Stl'atl'imx Resource Use*. Vancouver: UBC Press.

Hebda, R.J., N.J. Turner, S. Birchwater, M. Kay and the Elders of Ulkatcho: Andrew Cahoose, Andy Cahoose, Annie Cahoose, Lashaway Cahoose, Mary Joe Cahoose, Peter Cahoose, Wilfred Cassam, Eddie Elkins, Henry Jack, Maddie Jack, Mary Jack, Eliza Leon, Kelly Moffat, Marvin Paul, Frank Sill, Monica Sill, Andrew Squinas, Helen Squinas, Mack Squinas, Eustine Squinas,

Thomas Squinas, Lucy Sulin, Willie Sulin and Pierre West. 1996. *Ulkatcho Food and Medicine Plants.* Anahim Lake, B.C.: Ulkatcho Publishing.

Hitchcock, C.L., A. Cronquist, M. Ownbey, and J.W. Thompson. 1955-69. *Vascular Plants of the Pacific Northwest,* Parts 1-5. Seattle: University of Washington Press.

Honigmann, J.J. 1946. *Ethnography and Acculturation of the Fort Nelson Slave.* Publications in Anthropology, no. 33. New Haven, Conn.: Yale University Press.

Hultén, E. 1968. *Flora of Alaska and Neighboring Territories.* Stanford, Calif.: Stanford University Press.

Hunn, E.S. 1981. On the relative contribution of men and women to subsistence among hunter-gatherers of the Columbia Plateau: a comparison with ethnographic atlas summaries. *Journal of Ethnobiology* 1:1:124-34.

Hunn, E.S., and D.H. French. 1981. Lomatium. A key resource for Columbia Plateau native subsistence. *Northwest Science* 55:2: 87-94.

Hunn, E.S., and J. Selam and family. 1990. *Nch'i-Wana. "The Big River". Mid-Columbia Indians and Their Land.* Seattle: University of Washington Press.

Hunn, E.S., N.J. Turner, and D.H. French. In press. Ethnobiology and subsistence. In *Plateau,* edited by D.E. Walker. Vol. 12, *Handbook of North American Indians,* edited by W.C. Sturtevant. Washington, D.C.: Smithsonian Institution.

Johnson, D., L. Kershaw, A. MacKinnon and J. Pojar. 1995. *Plants of the Western Boreal Forest and Aspen Parkland.* Edmonton: Lone Pine Publishing; Ottawa: Canadian Forest Service.

Johnston, A. 1970. Blackfoot Indian utilization of the flora of the northwestern Great Plains. *Economic Botany* 24:3:301-324.

Kari, P.R. 1987. *Tanaina Plantlore. Dena'ina K'et'una. An Ethnobotany of the Dena'ina Indians of Southcentral Alaska.* Anchorage: National Park Service, Alaska Region.

Kay, Michèle. 1995. Environmental, cultural and linguistic factors affecting Ulkatcho (Carrier) botanical knowledge. Master's thesis, Department of Biology, University of Victoria, Victoria.

Kingsbury, J.M. 1964. *Poisonous Plants of the United States and Canada.* Englewood Cliffs, N.J.: Prentice-Hall.

Kruckeberg, A.R. 1982. *Gardening with Native Plants of the Pacific Northwest.* Vancouver: Douglas & McIntyre.

'Ksan, People of the. 1980. *Gathering What the Great Nature Provided. Food Traditions of the Gitksan.* Vancouver: Douglas & McIntyre;

Seattle: University of Washington Press.

Kuhnlein, H.V., and N.J. Turner. 1987. Cow-parsnip (*Heracleum lanatum* Michx.): an indigenous vegetable of Native people of northwestern North America. *Journal of Ethnobiology* 6:2:309-24.

———. 1991. *Traditional Plant Foods of Canadian Indigenous Peoples: Nutrition, Botany and Use.* Vol. 8, *Food and Nutrition in History and Anthropology*, edited by Solomon Katz. Philadelphia: Gordon and Breach Science Publishers.

Laforet, A., N.J. Turner and A. York. 1993. Traditional foods of the Fraser Canyon Nlaka'pamux. In *American Indian Linguistics and Ethnography in Honor of Laurence C. Thompson*, edited by A. Mattina and T. Montler. University of Montana Occasional Papers in Linguistics no. 10. Missoula: University of Montana Press.

Leighton, A.L. 1985. *Wild Plant Use by the Woods Cree (Nihithawak) of East-Central Saskatchewan.* Mercury Series Paper 101, Canadian Ethnology Service. Hull, Quebec: Canadian Museum of Civilization.

Lepofsky, D.L., K. Kusmer, B. Hayden and K.P. Lertzman. 1996. Reconstructing prehistoric socioeconomies from palaeoethnobotanical and zooarchaeological data: an example from the British Columbia plateau. *Journal of Ethnobiology* 16:1:31-62.

Lyons, C.P., and B. Merilees. 1995. *Trees, Shrubs and Flowers to Know in British Columbia and Washington.* Edmonton: Lone Pine Publishing.

MacKinnon, A., J. Pojar and R. Coupé, eds. 1992. *Plants of Northern British Columbia.* Edmonton: Lone Pine Publishing; Victoria: British Columbia Ministry of Forests.

Marles, R.J. 1984. The ethnobotany of the Chipewyan of northern Saskatchewan. Masters thesis, Department of Biology, University of Saskatchewan, Saskatoon.

McNeary, S. 1974. The traditional economic and social life of the Niska of British Columbia. Unpublished report to the National Museum of Canada.

Medical Services, Pacific Region. 1971. *Indian Food.* Ottawa: Health and Welfare Canada.

Meidinger, D., and J. Pojar. 1991. *Ecosystems of British Columbia.* Special Report Series 6. Victoria: British Columbia Ministry of Forests, Research Branch.

Meilleur, B.A., E.S. Hunn, R.L. Cox. 1990. *Lomatium dissectum* (Apiaceae): Multi-purpose plant of the Pacific Northwest. *Journal of Ethnobiology* 10:10: 1-20.

Morice, Rev. Father A.G. (OMI). 1893. *Notes Archaeological, Industrial and Sociological on the Western Dénés.* Transactions of the Canadian Institute, vol. 4.

Mourning Dove. 1933. How Coyote happened to make the Black Moss food. In *Coyote Stories.* Caldwell, Idaho: Caxton Printers.

Norton, H.H., E.S. Hunn, C.S. Martinsen and P.B. Keely. 1984. Vegetable food products of the foraging economies of the Pacific Northwest. *Ecology of Food and Nutrition* 14:219-28.

Palmer, G. 1975. Shuswap Indian ethnobotany. *Syesis* 8:29-81.

Parish, R., R. Coupé and D. Lloyd, eds. 1996. *Plants of the Southern Interior of British Columbia.* Edmonton: Lone Pine Publishing; Victoria: British Columbia Ministry of Forests.

Peacock, S. In press. Putting down roots: the archaeology and ethnobotany of traditional root resource use on the Canadian plateau. In *The Archaeobotany of Hunter-Gatherers in Temperate Regions,* edited by J. Hather and S. Mason. London: Institute of Archaeology.

Perry, F. 1952. Ethno-botany of the Indians in the interior of British Columbia. *Museum Notes* 2:36-43.

Pokotylo, D.L., and P.D. Froese. 1983. Archaeological evidence for prehistoric root gathering on the southern Interior Plateau of British Columbia: a case study from upper Hat Creek valley. *Canadian Journal of Archaeology* 7:2: 127-57.

Spier, L., ed. 1938. *The Sinkaietk or Southern Okanagan of Washington.* Contributions from the Laboratory of Anthropology 2, General Series in Anthropology, no. 6. Menasha, Wisconsin: George Banta Publishing Company.

Steedman, E.V., ed. 1930. The ethnobotany of the Thompson Indians of British Columbia. [Based on James Teit's field-notes.] In *Bureau of American Ethnology, 45th Annual Report,* 1927-28. Washington, D.C.: Smithsonian Institution.

Stubbs, R.D. 1966. *An Investigation of the Edible and Medicinal Plants Used by the Flathead Indians.* Master's thesis. University of Montana.

Surtees, U. (with Mary Thomas). 1974. *Lak-la Hai-ee: Interior Salish Food Preparation.* Kelowna, B.C.: Lamont-Surtees Publishing.

Szczawinski, A.F. 1962. *The Heather Family of British Columbia.* Handbook no. 19. Victoria: British Columbia Provincial Museum.

Szczawinski, A.F., and G.A. Hardy. 1971. *Guide to Common Edible Plants of British Columbia.* Handbook no. 20. Victoria: British Columbia Provincial Museum.

Taylor, T.M.C. 1956. *The Ferns and Fern-allies of British Columbia.* Handbook no. 12. Victoria British Columbia Provincial Museum.

———. 1966. *The Lily Family of British Columbia.* Handbook no. 25. Victoria: British Columbia Provincial Museum.

———. 1973. *The Rose Family of British Columbia.* Handbook no. 30. Victoria: British Columbia Provincial Museum.

———. 1974. *The Pea Family of British Columbia.* Handbook no. 32. Victoria: British Columbia Provincial Museum.

Teit, J.A. 1900. *The Thompson Indians.* Memoir no. 2. New York: American Museum of Natural History.

———. 1906A. *The Lillooet Indians.* Memoir no. 4. New York: American Museum of Natural History.

———. 1906B. Notes on the Tahltan Indians of British Columbia. In *Boas Anniversary Volume.* New York: American Museum of Natural History.

———. 1909. *The Shuswap.* Memoir no. 5. New York: American Museum of Natural History.

———. 1930. The Salishan tribes of the western plateaus. In *Bureau of American Ethnology, 45th Annual Report,* 1927-28. Washington, D.C.: Smithsonian Institution. [Note: James Teit's ethnographic work was carried out under the direction of Franz Boas. His writings, including the five preceding publications, contain some of the earliest descriptions of plant foods of Interior First Peoples. His detailed ethnobotanical work with the Nlaka'pamux is published in a work edited by Elsie Steedman (1930).]

Thoms, A.V. 1989. The northern roots of hunter-gatherer intensification: camas and the Pacific Northwest. Ph.D. diss., Dept of Anthropology, Washington State University, Pullman.

Turner, N.J. 1973. The ethnobotany of the Bella Coola Indians of British Columbia. *Syesis* 6:193-220.

———. 1974. Plant taxonomic systems and ethnobotany of three contemporary Indian groups of the Pacific Northwest (Haida, Bella Coola and Lillooet). *Syesis* 7 (sup. 1).

———. 1977. Economic importance of Black Tree Lichen (*Bryoria fremontii*) to the Indians of western North America. *Economic Botany* 31:461-70.

———. 1979. *Plants in British Columbia Indian Technology.* Handbook no. 38. Victoria: British Columbia Provincial Museum

———. 1981a. A gift for the taking: the untapped potential of some food plants of North American native peoples. *Canadian Journal of Botany* 59:11:2331-57.

Turner, N.J. 1981b. Indian use of *Shepherdia canadensis* (Soapberry) in western North America. *Davidsonia* 12:1:1-14.

——. 1988. "The importance of a rose." Evaluating the cultural significance of plants in Thompson and Lillooet Interior Salish. *American Anthropologist* 90:2:272-90.

——. 1991a. Wild berries. In *Berries*, edited by J. Bennett. Toronto: Harrowsmith Books.

——. 1991b. Burning mountain sides for better crops: aboriginal landscape burning in British Columbia. *Archaeology in Montana* 32:2 (special issue). Excerpts reprinted in *International Journal of Ecoforestry* 10:3:116-22.

——. 1992. Plant resources of the Stl'atl'imx (Fraser River Lillooet) people: a window into the past. In *Complex Cultures of the British Columbia Plateau: Traditional Stl'atl'imx Resource Use*, edited by B. Hayden. Vancouver: UBC Press.

——. 1995. *Food Plants of Coastal First Peoples*. Royal British Columbia Museum Handbook. Vancouver; UBC Press; Victoria: Royal British Columbia Museum.

——. 1996. Traditional ecological knowledge. In *The Rain Forests of Home. Profile of a North American Bioregion*. Edited by P.K. Schoonmaker, B. von Hagen and E.C. Wolf, Ecotrust. Covelo, California, and Washington, D.C.: Island Press.

Turner, N.J., and M.A.M. Bell. 1971. The ethnobotany of the Coast Salish Indians of Vancouver Island. *Economic Botany* 25:1:63-104.

——. 1973. The Ethnobotany of the Southern Kwakiutl Indians of British Columbia. *Economic Botany* 27:3:257-310.

Turner, N.J., R. Bouchard, and D.I.D. Kennedy. 1980. *The Ethnobotany of the Okanagan-Colville Indians of British Columbia and Washington*. Victoria: British Columbia Provincial Museum.

Turner, N.J., and A. Davis. 1993. "When everything was scarce." The role of plants as famine foods in northwestern North America. *Journal of Ethnobiology* 13:2:1-28.

Turner, N.J., H.V. Kuhnlein and K.N. Egger. 1985. The Cottonwood Mushroom: a food resource of the Interior Salish Indian peoples of British Columbia. *Canadian Journal of Botany* 65:921-27.

Turner, N.J., and A.F. Szczawinski. 1991. *Common Poisonous Plants and Mushrooms of North America*. Portland: Timber Press.

Turner, N.J., L.C. Thompson, M.T. Thompson and A.Z. York. 1990. *Thompson Ethnobotany: Knowledge and Usage of Plants by the Thompson Indians of British Columbia*. Victoria: Royal British Columbia Museum.

Walker, D.E., ed. In press. *Plateau*. Vol. 12, *Handbook of North American Indians*, edited by W.C. Sturtevant. Washington, D.C.: Smithsonian Institution.

Yanovsky, E., and R.M. Kingsbury. 1938. Analyses of some Indian food plants. *Journal of the Association of Official Agricultural Chemists* 21:4:648-65.

INDEX

S

Saccharin, Wild   90, 91
Sagebrush, Big   13, 188
Sagebrush Mariposa   64
Sagittaria cuneata   160
　　latifolia   **160**
Salal   **162**
Salix exigua   189
salmon   15, 19, 30, 31, 35, 62, 67,
　　74, 85, 88, 104, 111, 117, 128,
　　141, 143, 148, 180
salmon eggs (roe)   27, 35, 74, 85,
　　88, 112, 148
Salmonberry   152, **164**
Salsify   189
Sambucus cerulea   **103-4**
　　glauca   103
　　pubens   103
　　racemosa   **103-4**
Saskatoon Berry   7, 20, 24, 25, 27,
　　29, 30, 31, 35, 52, 62, 74, 89,
　　94, 102, 105, 107, 109, 110,
　　128, 138, **139-41**, 163, 185
Scirpus acutus   189
seaweed   9, 31, 159
Seaweed, Edible   159
Sedum divergens   **162**
Self-heal   **168**
Service Berry   139
Shad-bush   139
Shaggy Mane   38, **40**
Shepherdia canadensis   **108-10**
Shepherd's Purse   **173**
Silverberry   25, **167**
Silverweed, Common   **145**
Sium suave   **90-91**
Skunk Cabbage   **59-60**
Smilacina racemosa   **75-76**
　　stellata   **75-76**
Snowberry   184
Snowberry, Creeping   **113**
Snowbush   **168**
Snowdrop, Yellow   71
Soapberry   15, 20, 24, 29, 30, 31,
　　105, **108-10**, 141

Solanum tuberosum   **177**
Solomon's Seal, False   35, **75-76**,
　　166, 179
　　Star-flowered   **75-76**
Soopolallie   108
Sorbus sitchensis   **164**
Sorrel, Sheep   175
Sour-grass   **175**
Spatlum   136
sphagnum   114, 121, 123
Spiraea   **169**
Spiraea pyramidata   **169**
Spitlum   136
Spring Beauty   7, 25, 68, 72,
　　133-35, 139, 177;
　　see also Potato, Indian
Spruce, Black   **165**
　　Engelmann   14, 188
　　White   14, 15, 25, 165, 189
squash, cultivated   **174**
Squashberry   105
squirrels   27, 52, 56, 57, 100
Stenanthium occidentale   **178**
Stonecrop   **162**
Stoneseed, Long-flowered   **166**
strawberries, cultivated   143, **175**
　　wild   6, 21, 29, **143-44**, 152,
　　153, 156, 175
Strawberry, Blue-leaf   **143-44**
　　Tall   **143-44**
Strawberry Blite   **185-86**
Streptopus amplexifolius   **179**
　　streptopoides   **179**
sugar   19, 20, 31, 35, 51, 67, 71, 79,
　　93, 94, 96, 107, 109, 110, 115,
　　141, 162
sugar, Douglas-fir   21, 35, 57-58
Sumac   183, 189
Sunflower   **172**, 173
Sunflower, Spring   92
　　Wild   92
Swamp Lantern   59
Sweet Root   88
Symphoricarpos albus   **184-85**
　　occidentalis   **184-85**

The cover photographs and all the photographs in this book were taken by and © by R.D. and N.J. Turner, except for the following:

page 76: photographed by A. Bernand, © A. Bernand, reprinted with permission;

pages 40, 116, 122, 131, 151 (top) and 178: photographed by W. van Dieren, © Royal British Columbia Museum;

page 21: photographer unknown, © Royal British Columbia Museum; and

pages 22 and 58: photographer(s) unknown, from Davidson 1915 and 1919, respectively.

The map on page 18 is reproduced courtesy of the Museum of Anthropology, University of British Columbia.

This edition was edited, designed and typeset by Gerry Truscott, RBCM. Set entirely in Baskerville (body text: 10/12).

Inside photographic production by Andrew Niemann, RBCM.
Cover design by Chris Tyrrell, RBCM.
Printed by Friesens, Winnipeg, Manitoba.